CREATIVE
HOMEOWNER®

FENCES
& GATES
PLAN ▪ DESIGN ▪ BUILD

CREATIVE HOMEOWNER®, Upper Saddle River, New Jersey

Editorial Director: Timothy O. Bakke
Production Manager: Kimberly H. Vivas

Senior Editor: Mike McClintock
Assistant Editor: Daniel Lane
Editorial Assistants: Dan Houghtaling,
    Sharon Ranftle
Copy Editor: Bruce Wetterau
Photo Researcher: Sharon Ranftle
Technical Consultant: Dave Thompson
Indexer: Sandi Schroeder

Senior Designer: Glee Barre
Cover Design: Clarke Barre
Illustrations: Michael Gellatly, Glee Barre
How-To Photography: Freeze Frame Studio
Additional How-to Photography: Brian C. Nieves,
    John Parsekian
Photo Assistants: Frank Krumrie, Dan Lane,
    Margaret McGill

Manufactured in the United States of America

Current Printing (last digit)
10 9 8 7 6 5 4

Fences and Gates
Library of Congress Catalog Card Number:
2001090506
ISBN: 1-58011-094-0

CREATIVE HOMEOWNER®
A Division of Federal Marketing Corp.
24 Park Way, Upper Saddle River, NJ 07458
www.creativehomeowner.com

Safety

Although the methods in this book have been reviewed for safety, it is not possible to overstate the importance of using the safest methods you can. What follows are reminders—some do's and don'ts of work safety—to use along with your common sense.

- Always use caution, care, and good judgment when following the procedures described in this book.
- Always be sure that the electrical setup is safe, that no circuit is overloaded, and that all power tools and outlets are properly grounded. Do not use power tools in wet locations.
- Always read container labels on paints, solvents, and other products; provide ventilation; and observe all other warnings.
- Always read the manufacturer's instructions for using a tool, especially the warnings.
- Use hold-downs and push sticks whenever possible when working on a table saw. Avoid working short pieces if you can.
- Always remove the key from any drill chuck (portable or press) before starting the drill.
- Always pay deliberate attention to how a tool works so that you can avoid being injured.
- Always know the limitations of your tools. Do not try to force them to do what they were not designed to do.
- Always check that any adjustment is locked before proceeding. For example, always check the rip fence on a table saw or the bevel adjustment on a portable saw before starting to work.
- Always clamp small pieces to a bench or other work surface when using a power tool.

- Always wear the appropriate rubber gloves or work gloves when handling chemicals, moving or stacking lumber, working with concrete, or doing heavy construction.
- Always wear a disposable face mask when you create dust by sawing or sanding. Use a special filtering respirator when working with toxic substances and solvents.
- Always wear eye protection, especially when using power tools or striking metal on metal or concrete; a chip can fly off, for example, when chiseling concrete.
- Never work while wearing loose clothing, open cuffs, or jewelry; tie back long hair.
- Always be aware that there is seldom enough time for your body's reflexes to save you from injury from a power tool in a dangerous situation; everything happens too fast. Be alert!
- Always keep your hands away from the business ends of blades, cutters, and bits.
- Always hold a circular saw firmly, usually with both hands.
- Always use a drill with an auxiliary handle to control the torque when using large-size bits.
- Always check your local building codes when planning new construction. The codes are intended to protect public safety and should be observed to the letter.

- Never work with power tools when you are tired or when under the influence of alcohol or drugs.
- Never cut tiny pieces of wood, vinyl, metal, or pipe using a power saw. When you need a smaller piece, saw it from a securely clamped longer piece.
- Never change a saw blade or a drill or router bit unless the power cord is unplugged. Do not depend on the switch being off. You might accidentally hit it.
- Never work in insufficient lighting.
- Never work with dull tools. Have them sharpened, or learn how to sharpen them yourself.
- Never use a power tool on a workpiece—large or small—that is not firmly supported.
- Never saw a workpiece that spans a large distance between horses without close support on each side of the cut; the piece can bend, closing on and jamming the blade, causing saw kickback.
- When sawing, never support a workpiece from underneath with your leg or any other part of your body.
- Never carry sharp or pointed tools or materials, such as utility knives, awls, or chisels, in your pocket. If you want to conveniently carry any of these tools, use a special-purpose tool belt that has leather pockets and holders.

Contents

Introduction

Introduction

For thousands of years fences have been used to contain livestock or provide privacy and security. Today fences are not only for keeping things in or out of your yard but also for beautifying the exterior of your home. Most modern fences are designed to be beautiful as well as useful. Even an attractive, low picket fence provides a degree of security and will prevent your pets from leaving your yard. This book will show you that when it comes to fences, you need not trade aesthetics for utility.

Guide to Skill Level
Look for these estimates of job difficulty.

ONE
Easy, even for beginners

TWO
Challenging. Can be done by beginners who have the patience and willingness to learn.

THREE
Difficult. Can be done by experienced do-it-yourselfers who have mastered basic construction skills and have the tools and time for the job.

Site Planning

Design Options

Before you start digging fence holes, bear in mind that building codes and zoning ordinances do not always favor a homeowner's desire for privacy, at least not when it comes to outdoor spaces.

In many areas there are rules about building any permanent structure close to your property line and about height restrictions on a fence no matter where you build it. Some areas (mainly in zones with old or historic buildings) even have restrictions on what materials and colors you can use.

There are exceptions to every rule. But the official version, called a variance, can be a drawn-out and difficult process. You may have to submit multiple copies of your plans to the building department or planning board, post notices, and attend public meetings where neighbors can object to your fence design or location.

If you're looking for privacy or protection from street noise, you could opt for a dense line of trees and shrubs. An interlocking line of foliage does a good job of screening out sights and sounds. But unless you spend thousands for mature plantings, you'll have to wait years for the natural fence to fill in.

Filling between Posts

Solid walls can create outdoor rooms nearly as private as the ones inside. You can make them out of bricks or blocks and face them in stucco or stone. But their great weight requires a masonry foundation, which means heavy-duty excavation and concrete work before you start on the wall.

It's much easier to build a screening fence anchored by 4x4 posts every 6 to 8 feet. The posts can support rails and a series of boards, slats, lattice, or pickets to form either a partial screen or a full screen that shields an outdoor space.

The covering on the basic fence frame is the most adjustable part of the design. You can select different types of wood and different widths, set the boards at angles, and increase or decrease the spacing between boards. Each change has a different effect on the overall appearance of the fence and on the amount of wind protection, shade, and privacy.

Even if you have a particular type of wood and fence pattern in mind, take the time to clamp a few boards in place to be sure that the spacing gives you the desired degree of privacy.

Fence Fillers

Once you have erected and braced the basic structural grid of posts and rails, you can add a variety of screening fillers. There are so many options that it's best to experiment. For example, you could tack vertical slats between the top and bottom connectors or horizontal slats between posts.

The screening boards could be set plumb or diagonal and very close together for the most privacy or far-

Layout

To visualize your fence plan, measure out from the house or nearby lot boundaries to establish straight lines.

You can mark the layout with chalk or use a long extension cord that you can adjust to mark different plans.

Wind

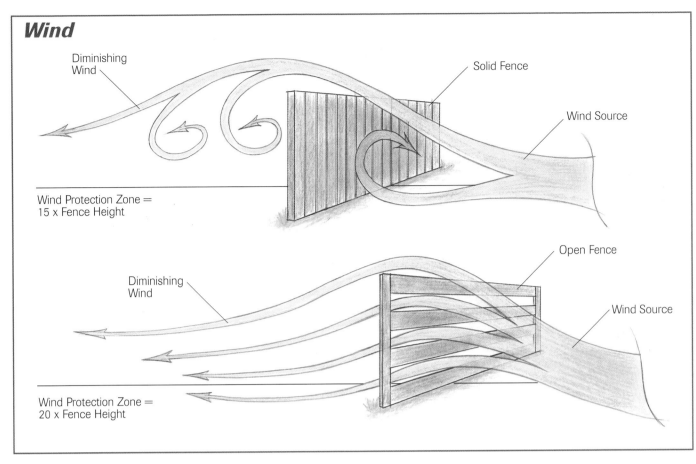

Diminishing
Wind

Solid Fence

Wind Source

Wind Protection Zone =
15 x Fence Height

Diminishing
Wind

Open Fence

Wind Source

Wind Protection Zone =
20 x Fence Height

Sun and Shade

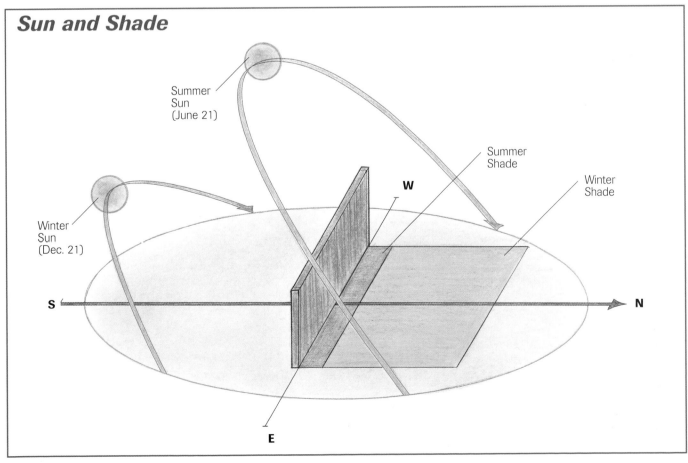

Summer
Sun
(June 21)

Summer
Shade

Winter
Shade

Winter
Sun
(Dec. 21)

W

S

N

E

ther apart in a sun-drenched yard to let in more breeze or preserve more of the view.

If privacy fences were adjustable (like the strips of glass in a jalousie window), you could adjust the slats to match the degree of privacy you wanted. And, in theory, you could build such a fence, using jalousie hardware mounted on the sides of the posts fitted with thin wooden slats instead of glass.

The Degree of Privacy

You can start with a very open design using one of the fence boards as a spacer between the components. Leaving gaps that are wider than a board generally has a marginal effect. Then try sliding the pieces closer together, leaving gaps that are about half as wide as the width of each board.

Also experiment with different patterns. Try setting boards on the diagonal or even in a V-pattern between the posts. You can use lumber ranging from 1x2s to 1x6s, generally with one size but also in combinations of sizes.

Although the installation is more time consuming, you can install boards at an angle so that from one side of the yard you would see the faces head on. From that vantage point, the boards would appear to be overlapped, creating complete privacy. But from the opposite side of the yard you would see only the narrow edges of the boards and through the spaces between them, creating only a partial screen.

If possible, also experiment with the effects of moving the fence toward or away from the area you want to protect. This can alter the overall sense of privacy as much as the space you leave between boards.

In general, the closer you are to the fence, the easier it is to see through it. The view may be interrupted by fence components, but it's easy to assemble the fragmented views into a comprehensive picture. The farther you are from the fence, the harder it is to see what's happening behind it. So if you want to preserve your long-range view, a good design would use an open board pattern in a fence built close to the private area but far from the nearest vantage point.

The best approach is to try several plans, tacking the boards with finishing nails and observing the effects of different angles and spacing from different areas of the yard. You can sketch out different plans on paper, but trial and error is the best way to find the best balance between openness and seclusion.

Cutting and Shaping Boards

Decorative fences with unusual crisscross shapes, curves, and cutouts can look spectacular. But woodworking time can mushroom when you have to create the decorative details again and again on every board. In general, it's wise to use stock-size lumber and make cuts to length with a circular saw (near right). If you do want to add accents, such as a cutout in a picket, make a template or holding jig that allows you to mass-produce the detail without measuring from scratch each time. Curves take the most time because you have to cut them with a saber saw (far right). To create a contour on many components, cut one, check to make sure it fits properly, and save the piece to use as a cutting template.

Angle Effect on Privacy

Minimum

Spacing Effect on Privacy

Minimum

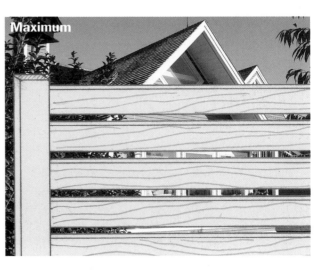

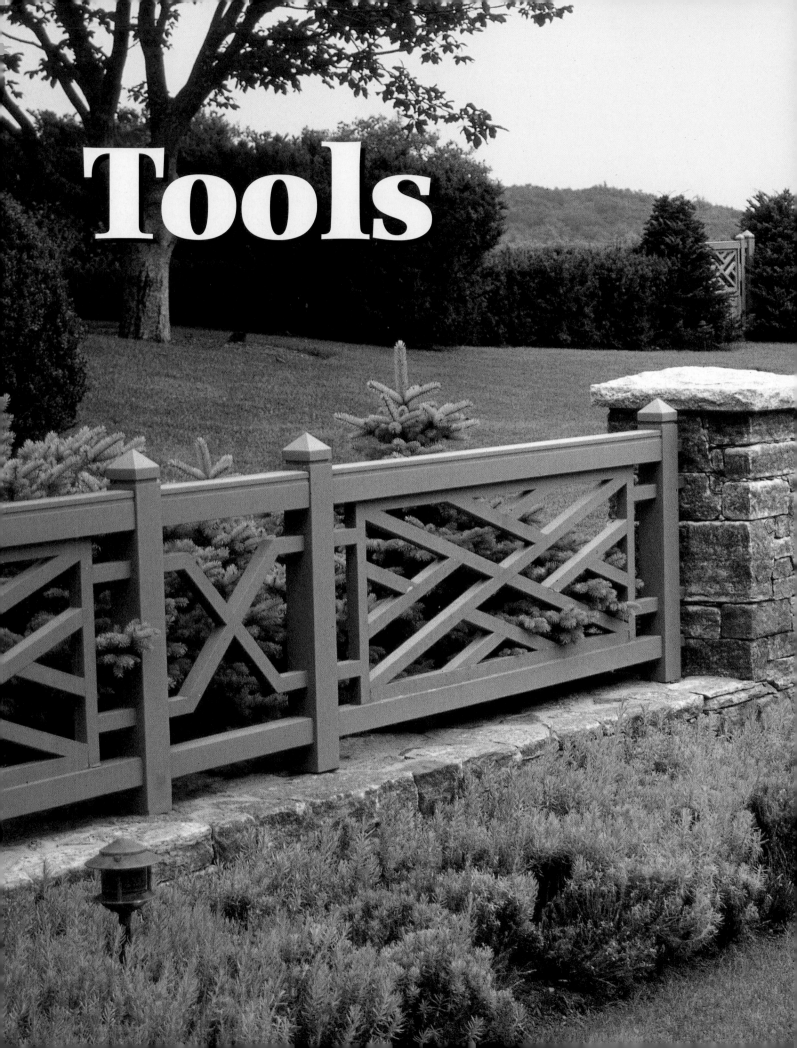

Tools

Layout and Excavation

A basic collection of rulers, squares, and levels should serve on a typical fence project. Note that it always helps to follow the adage "Measure twice and cut once," particularly when it can save an extra trip to the lumberyard for more wood.

For measuring, you can use a classic carpenter's fold-out ruler or a measuring tape. The fold-out variety takes a little time to open and close, but some models have a handy pull-out extension that makes it easy to take accurate inside dimensions.

To square up measurements for cutting, use a combination square on smaller boards and a framing square on sheet materials. But you can also check for square by measuring the diagonals between posts. They should be equal if the posts are square.

Another trick that's good for fence corners is to use the proportions of a 3-4-5 triangle. If one leg is 3 feet long, another is 4 feet long, and the hypotenuse is 5 feet long, the angle between the two legs will be 90 degrees. The 3-4-5 system works at any scale.

Marking Boards

Combination squares mark straight, square lines.

Sliding T-bevels mark and transfer odd angles.

Layout Tools

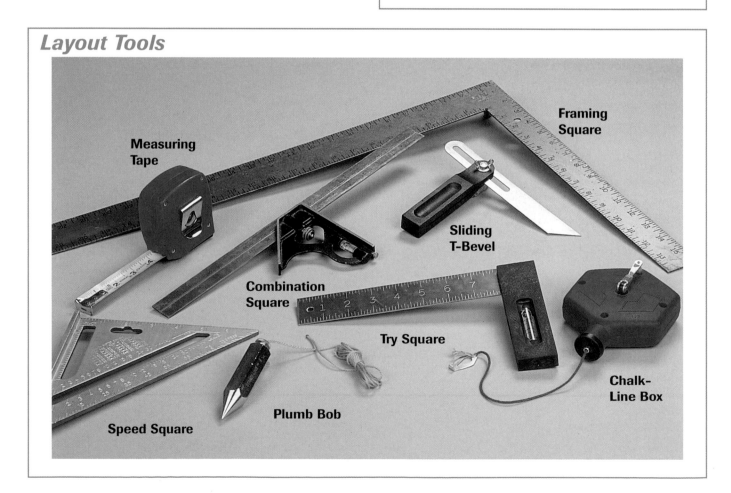

Measuring Tape

Framing Square

Combination Square

Sliding T-Bevel

Try Square

Speed Square

Plumb Bob

Chalk-Line Box

Excavation Tools

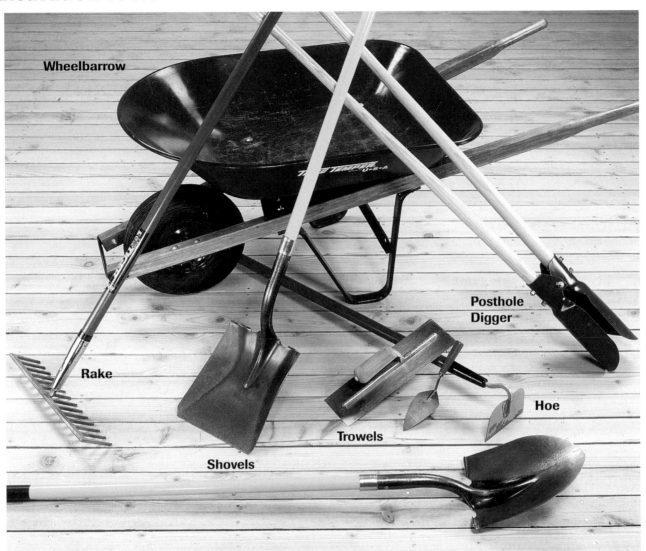

Wheelbarrow

Rake

Shovels

Trowels

Posthole Digger

Hoe

Water Level

One of the simplest and most inexpensive tools used in fence work, a water level is also one of the most practical and accurate. It works just as well as an exotic laser level but uses only water and requires no special handling or calibration. The tool consists of a length of clear plastic tubing. It can be as long as you need it to be and can run up and down over rough terrain between posts. The red color in the tube (right) comes from dye that's included in some water-level kits to make it easier to read. Kits also contain clips for holding the tubing. Because water always seeks its own level, once you make sure there are no air bubbles in the line, the water at one end of the tube will be level with water at the other end.

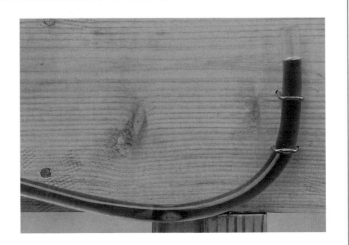

Construction Tools

Many do-it-yourselfers already own the basic hand tools required for building fences and gates. Unless you plan a special application, such as a fence with boards and gates with highly detailed gingerbread trim, you won't need any specialized tools.

But if you are in the process of accumulating how-to tools, consider these general buying guidelines. Naturally, the selection that's right for you depends on the work you want to do, but also on how often you'll use the tools, how expert you are at handling them, and how much you want to spend.

■ **Durability.** Buy better quality in tools you'll use often, such as a hammer and saw, that are basic requirements for building a fence. It's worth a little extra to have a set of chisels with steel-capped heads that stand up better than plastic heads. But don't pay top dollar for heavy-duty, contractor tools you'll use only occasionally. Many have features you don't need. And the truth is that inexperienced do-it-yourselfers don't get professional results just by using top-notch tools. For the most part, skill is in the hand that holds them, not in the tools themselves.

■ **Precision.** Stick with basic tools designed to do one job well, and avoid multipurpose gimmick tools that are loaded with bells and whistles. That nine-in-one wrench may be handy in the car glove compartment but not so much on home-improvement projects.

■ **Strength.** Look for hammers, wrenches, pry bars, and other mainly metal tools that are drop-forged instead of cast metal. Casting can trap air bubbles in molten metal, creating weak spots that could cause the metal to fracture under stress. Drop-forging removes more bubbles and makes the metal stronger and safer to use. In general, when manufacturers take the time and money to drop-forge a tool and machine-grind its surface, they leave the fine-grained metal in plain view. Sometimes inferior cast tools are disguised with a coat of paint.

■ **Price.** If in doubt, avoid the most and least expensive models. The top end can have more capacity than you need, and the bottom end often has fundamental flaws that make work difficult—even for a novice. There are some exceptions, of course. For example, a throw-away brush is fine for slapping some stain on a rough fence post. You don't need a high-quality and high-priced sash paintbrush for the job.

Finally, be sure to wield the tool in the store, checking the feel and comfort, to see whether it seems controllable, too heavy, or too light. If you shop in a large outlet store where there are several brands of the same tool, try one against another.

It can be difficult to compare tools you can't normally test on the spot, such as power saws. But some tools you can test. Before you buy a level, for example, check three or four on the store floor or counter, and stack them on top of each other to see whether one has a bubble that is out of line with the others.

In the end, of course, careful measurements and layouts will do more than top-notch tools to make your fence project both good-looking and long lasting.

Smart Tip MARKING THE SITE FOR UTILITIES

Before you start digging holes for fence posts, check into the location of underground utility lines, such as a natural gas main or a sewer pipe. On a big fence project where you're using a contractor to do the digging, you should mark the locations of these lines ahead of time to avoid an accident. Even if you are renting a portable power auger and digging the holes yourself, you can't afford to accidentally puncture a gas line or short out underground electrical cables. Local utility companies have a record of the locations, and in many regions, a utility company representative will come to the site and help you locate underground lines, so you can mark them with flags.

Hand Tools

FASTENING

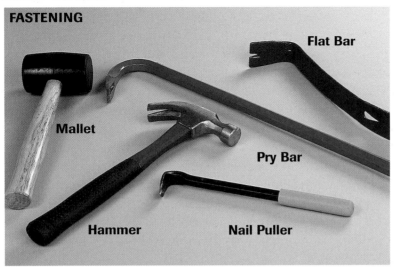

Mallet

Flat Bar

Hammer

Pry Bar

Nail Puller

SHAPING AND SMOOTHING

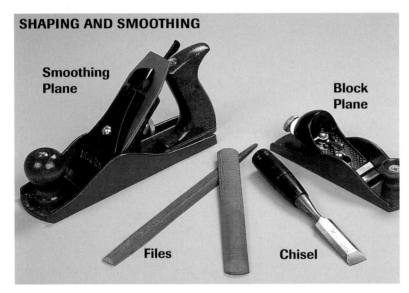

Smoothing Plane

Block Plane

Files

Chisel

LEVELING

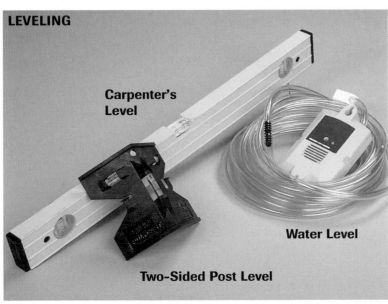

Carpenter's Level

Water Level

Two-Sided Post Level

Trimming Boards

You don't need to do much trimming and finishing on a rustic fence made of rough-sawn boards. But you may need to clean up a few edges on picket styles and other types of decorative fencing. A basic smoothing plane (top) works well on most wood, but to increase your production you can use a power planer (middle). A belt sander (bottom) makes quick work of rough spots and blemishes.

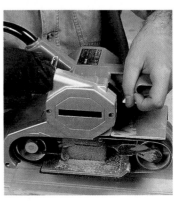

2 TOOLS

Power Tools and Safety Gear

A set of basic power tools will carry you through a typical fence-building project. With a lot of wood to cut, including posts, rails, and boards, you'll probably need a circular saw. The most practical is a standard corded model with a 7½-inch blade.

In remote locations, battery-powered saws (and other tools) will save you the trouble and tangle of extension cords. But on large projects you're likely to deplete the battery fairly quickly by cutting through thick posts. Even the latest battery-powered saws can't handle continuous production cutting as well as a corded saw can. To cut large posts you'll have to get the knack of making two passes from opposing sides because most saws don't have the blade diameter to cut completely through the wood.

To make a neat, nearly seamless combination of cuts, it helps to transfer the cut lines around the post with a combination square. Another option is to bury any rough cuts you make by eye in the ground and set the cleaner, factory-cut ends up.

Whenever possible, it's wise to make repetitive cuts ahead of time. You'll find that it's most economical to shape pickets, post tops, and such in a shop (or at least on stable sawhorses). Make cuts such as angled joints on mating boards in the field.

Power Tools

Drill-Driver

Circular Saw

Saber Saw

Reciprocating Saw

Pneumatic Nail Gun

With air-powered nailers you can load many nails in one clip (near right). Then position the tool and squeeze the trigger to drive them (far right). Once you get a feel for the tool, you'll be able to drive nails quickly and accurately, which is handy on a large fence project. And the tools are safe if handled properly. Check into the safety-head feature, which forces you to set the head firmly against the work before the trigger will fire a fastener.

Safety Equipment

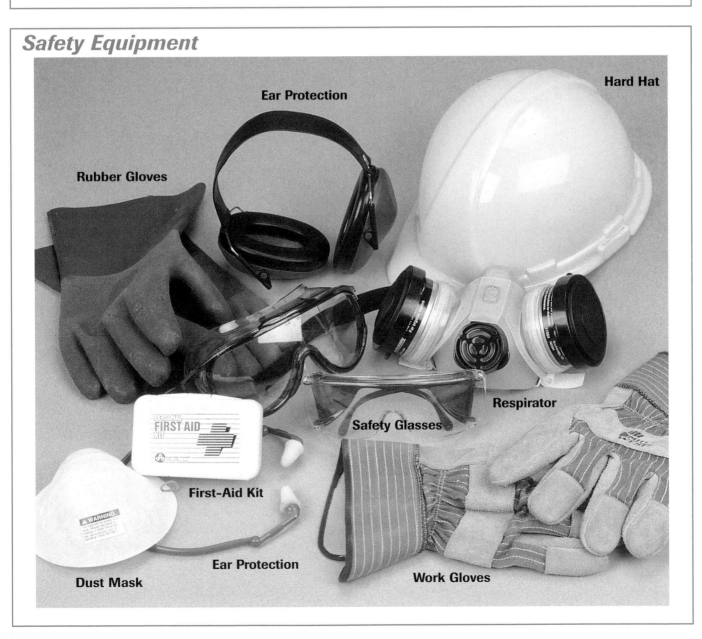

Ear Protection

Hard Hat

Rubber Gloves

Respirator

Safety Glasses

First-Aid Kit

Ear Protection

Work Gloves

Dust Mask

Specialty Tools and Techniques

Most of the tools you need to build fences are the standards of do-it-yourself carpentry, such as a circular saw, drill, level, and such. But there are a few items that you may not have in the toolbox.

Among the most unusual is a come-along, which is basically a ratchet-controlled winch that allows you to apply and maintain a lot of pressure on posts or fence sections. It's handy when you need to pull a section into plumb position. Most of these tools come with two lengths of metal cable and hooks at the ends. Loop one end around a fence post, and anchor the other end to a large tree or temporary stake. Then you can ratchet increasing tension on the cables.

You also may need more than a standard carpenter's level, which is the most practical tool for plumbing and leveling fence posts and short lengths of rail. To establish levels over greater distances you'll need string and a line level, or a water level.

When it comes to digging postholes, you have several options. Use a shovel if you're digging only a few holes, or consider a two-handled posthole digger. This tool allows you to dig holes that are not much larger than the posts. With a shovel, you'll have to dig a larger hole and move more dirt. For big projects, rent a gasoline-powered auger.

Using a Come-Along

Come-alongs have cables and hooks that you can loop around a fence section that needs straightening.

Cranking the handle turns a ratchet gear and applies tremendous pulling force through the cables.

Special Protection from PT Chemicals

Experts say that some wood-preserving chemicals in pressure-treated (PT) lumber can leach out of the wood. Even casual contact with PT wood may transfer some chemicals. The most controversial treatments are those containing arsenic: chromated copper arsenate (CCA), ammoniacal copper arsenate (ACA), and ammoniacal copper zinc arsenate (ACZA). If you work with PT lumber, even outside on a fence, wear gloves. If you cut or sand PT wood, also wear goggles and a dust mask or respirator. The Environmental Protection Agency recommends that after working with arsenic-treated wood, you should wash thoroughly before eating or drinking.

Bracing a Post

Attach an angled 2x4 to a ground stake, and clamp it to the post as you adjust the post into plumb position.

For accuracy, brace the post in two directions with the 2x4s at right angles. Screws make disassembly easy.

Digging Options

Using a shovel is the most basic way to dig piers. But you'll wind up moving more dirt than you need to.

A posthole digger has a scissor action to cut and scoop out dirt. It makes a neater, smaller hole.

You can rent a one- or two-person power auger. They churn through dirt but are a handful to operate.

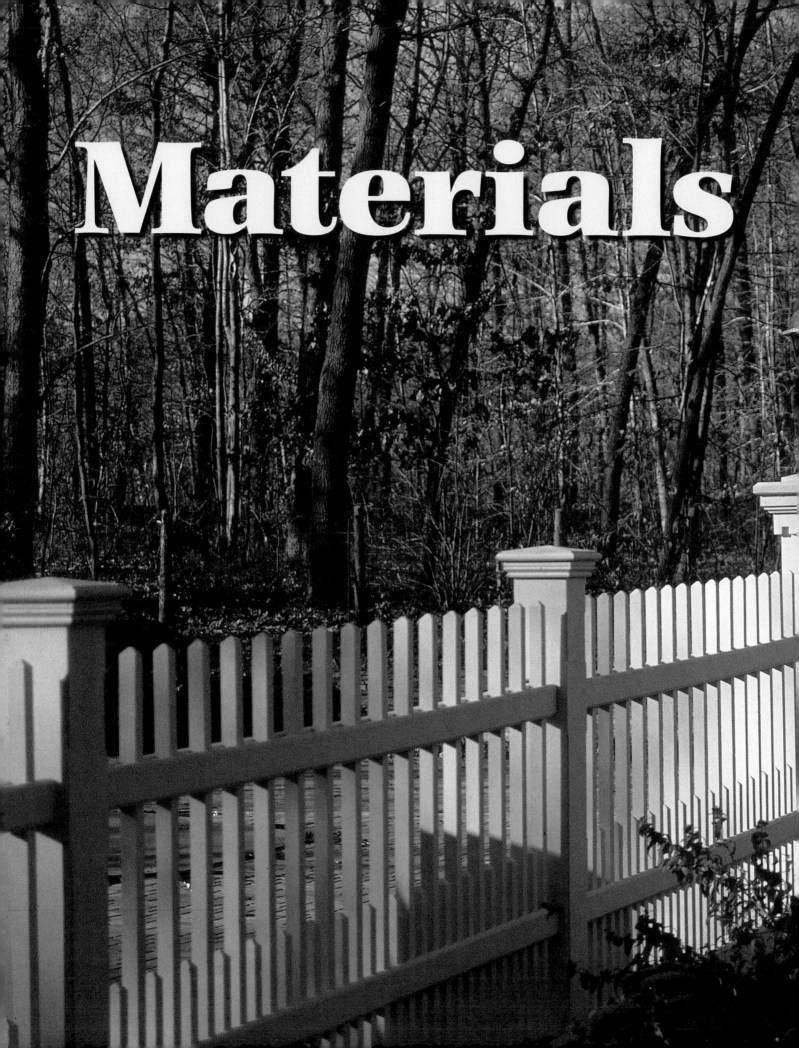

Materials

Fasteners

Besides common nails, which are the easiest to drive, you can use spiral or rink-shank nails on fence boards for more holding power. Although screws take more time to drive, they have the most holding power by far. A screw's number indicates the diameter of its shank. Common sizes are #6, #8, and #10. Of course, the length for any of these screws can vary. A #8 screw, for example, can be nearly any length up to about 3½ inches. The heavier the gauge, the more likely you are to find it in longer lengths.

You also may want to use large lag screws for making heavy-duty wood-to-wood attachments. Lag screws are heavy-duty screws that you drive with a socket wrench. Lags are sized according to the diameter of their shanks, usually ⁵⁄₁₆, ⅜, or ½ inch.

You can also use through bolts, mainly carriage bolts, which have unslotted oval heads, for attaching structural lumber face to face, such as large rails to posts. Carriage bolts have a square shoulder just beneath the head that digs into the wood as you tighten the bolt to prevent slipping. They are sized according to the diameter of their shanks as well as their length. You can also secure major joints between rails and posts with framing hardware, such as a U-shaped bracket that can support a heavy rail between posts. To prevent corrosion, hardware should be galvanized.

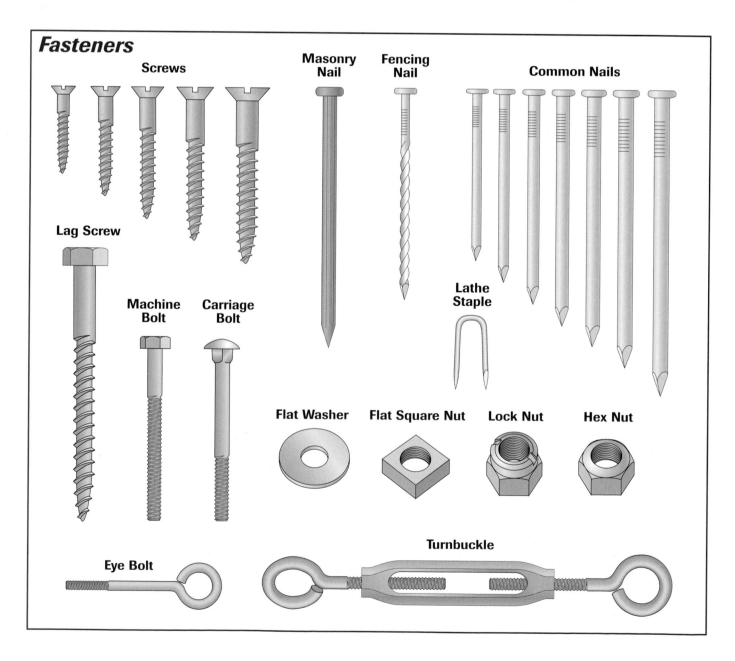

Fasteners

Screws • Masonry Nail • Fencing Nail • Common Nails • Lag Screw • Machine Bolt • Carriage Bolt • Lathe Staple • Flat Washer • Flat Square Nut • Lock Nut • Hex Nut • Eye Bolt • Turnbuckle

Posts

Many lumberyards stock several types of posts, including round posts and square timbers, generally sized 4x4 or 6x6. The selection may include redwood and cedar but often is limited to rough grades of fir and pressure-treated (PT) wood. PT wood is the most durable because it is infused under pressure with an insecticide and a fungicide to ward off pests and decay. Be sure to observe the warnings of the manufacturer.

6x6

4x4 Fir

4x4 PT

4x4 Cedar

Round Post

3 MATERIALS

Trim Posts

Large posts often are beyond the one-cut capacity of do-it-yourself circular saws and may be too thick for standard drill bits. But there are other options. One is to use a chain saw (observing manufacturer's cautions) or a reciprocating saw with a long wood-cutting blade. But most DIYers get by with squaring the cut line around the post and making two passes that meet in the middle. You can follow the same process when drilling holes, or use longer spade-point bits.

Board Options

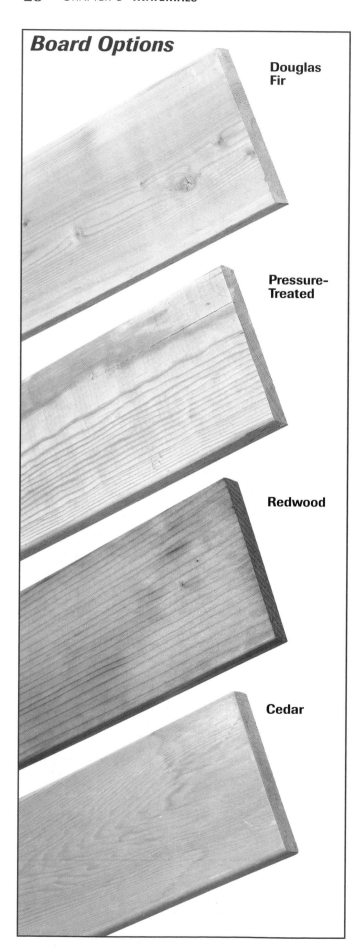

Douglas Fir

Pressure-Treated

Redwood

Cedar

Lumber

As with any organic material that gains and loses water, wood swells when it is moist and shrinks as it dries. This can lead to warping, checking, bowing, twisting, and cupping. Softwoods like pine, Douglas fir, and cedar are particularly vulnerable. But most of these problems can be avoided by fastening boards securely and supporting them with posts, rails, and braces over their spans.

When it comes to ordering posts, rails, and boards, bear in mind that a piece of lumber has two sizes: nominal and actual. A 2x4 rail may start out at 2x4 inches (its nominal size) when it is cut from a raw log, but it

Decay-Resistant Woods

Redwood and cedar are viable but pricey options to PT wood. Both combine good rot and insect resistance with an elegant appearance and are available in several grades. Less expensive grades with a rougher, saw-textured surface are generally used for fencing.

Redwood
- **Clear All Heart**
  Finest grade heartwood
- **Heart B**
  Limited knots
- **Clear (Sapwood)**
  Some defects
- **B Grade**
  Limited knots

Cedar
- **Clear Heart**
  Exposed wood
- **Grade A Clear**
  Shingles
- **Grade B Clear**
  Fencing
- **Knotty Grades**
  Closets

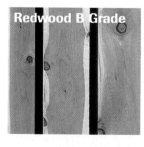

Redwood B Grade

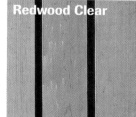

Redwood Clear

Cedar Grade B

Cedar Clear

soon shrinks when it is dried. Then it becomes even smaller when it is planed. A 2x4 soon becomes 1½ x 3½ inches—the lumber's actual size. For wood lengths, the nominal and actual lengths are almost always the same. When you buy a 10-foot 2x4, it is usually 10 feet long and sometimes a bit longer.

Some lumberyards charge for lumber by the board foot, though increasingly yards are charging by the individual stick, or piece of lumber. If your lumberyard charges you by the board foot, here's how to figure it: take the nominal thickness, multiply it by the nominal width and the length, and divide by 12. A 10-foot 2x6 (usually written 2x6x10' in the industry) would be 10 board feet.

Smart Tip   **WOOD STAMP**

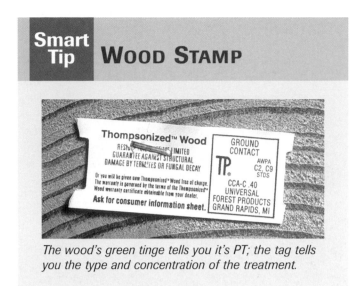

The wood's green tinge tells you it's PT; the tag tells you the type and concentration of the treatment.

Basic Lumber Grades

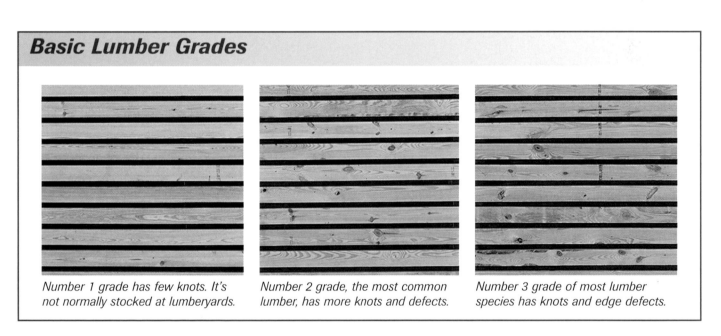

Number 1 grade has few knots. It's not normally stocked at lumberyards.

Number 2 grade, the most common lumber, has more knots and defects.

Number 3 grade of most lumber species has knots and edge defects.

Common Lumber Defects

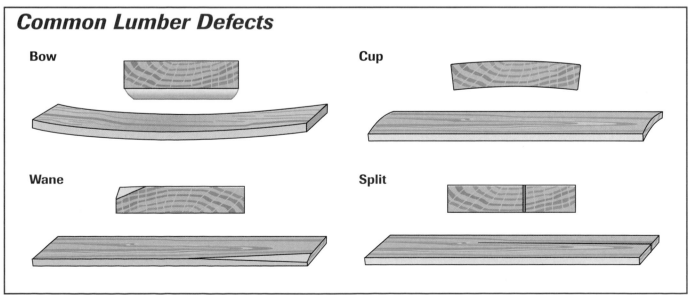

Bow

Cup

Wane

Split

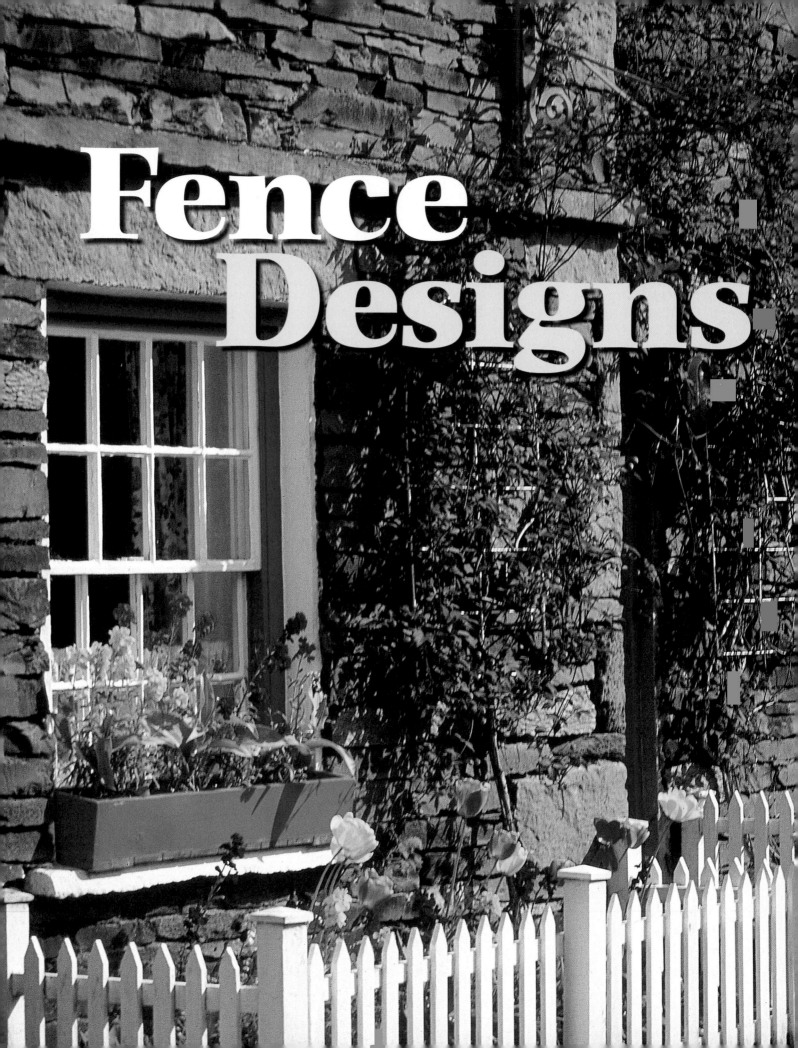

Fence Designs

Basic Post and Rail

The ideal location for a basic straight post-and-rail fence system is on relatively flat terrain and in a yard that can be bounded by square corners. Your situation may not be this accommodating. But by checking the photo sequence that includes all the important steps, you can lay out and build a good-looking and long-lasting fence. Here are some of the most important points you will need to know about.

■ Use a flexible marking system that allows you to make an accurate layout initially but doesn't get in the way of the digging—or become obliterated so that you can't relocate your post centers. One approach is to drive a stake a few feet past each end of a straight run. Brace the stake, and drive a nail to mark your centerline. String the line, and use it as a guide to mark post locations on the ground with chalk or spray paint. Remove the string while you dig, and string it again when it comes time to align the posts.

■ To double-check corners for square, use the 3-4-5 triangulation method. When you can connect the end points of 3-foot and 4-foot legs with a 5-foot hypotenuse, the corner is 90 degrees. Using large measuring units (feet instead of inches) produces the most accurate results.

■ Plan ahead of time to avoid odd-sized spaces between posts at the end of a run. This is a common

Fence Installation Overview

TOOLS
■ Sledgehammer
■ Hammer
■ Circular saw
■ Measuring tape

■ Safety glasses
■ Line level and
  4' spirit level
■ Drill with bit

MATERIALS
■ Mason's twine
■ 1x2s for stakes
■ 2x4s for batter boards
■ Nails

■ 4x4 posts
■ 2x4 rails
■ 1x4 pickets
■ 3" deck screws

1 ***Make your posts last longer*** *by applying preservative to the in-ground section, particularly the end grain.*

4 ***Set the lower rail on the nails,*** *check again for level, and mark the top and bottom of the rail on all the posts.*

5 ***Recess the rail*** *by cutting kerfs in the post equal to the depth of the rail. You can recess all or part of the rail.*

A basic straight fence with spaced pickets is a practical design and one of the easiest to build.

2 **To avoid using braces,** one basic approach is to compact the backfill as you plumb the post.

3 **Strike a level line** across the posts for the lower rail, and drive a temporary nail to mark its place.

6 **Use a hammer and chisel** to clear away the wood between the kerfs and flatten the base of the recess.

7 **Predrill at the ends of boards** to reduce the chance of splitting when you drive nails or screws.

4

FENCE DESIGNS

Continued on pg. 34

situation unless you divide the overall length of the fence into equal sections. Sometimes that works. But on shorter runs it can leave you with too much or too little space between posts. Remember that you want to get the most use from stock lengths of rails.

There are several ways around this problem. One is to use the most economical spacing on the main run and divide the remaining space equally for the last short runs to the end posts. Another approach is to bury an unequal run at a gate that you can build to take up the slack.

▪ Remember to allow for the thickness of lumber at corners. For example, if you want to turn the corner with rails, one will need to be a bit longer than the other to cover its end grain. Of course, you also can miter rails at corner posts.

▪ If you use prefabricated fence panels, locate post centers so that the panels either fit snugly between them or butt together on the centerline of the posts. The method you choose depends on the particular panel design; consult the manufacturer's instructions.

▪ Take the extra time required to predrill for nails or screws at the ends of boards. It's frustrating (and wastes time and material) to measure and cut a rail or cap piece to size only to have it split.

▪ Maintain even spacing between pickets or other boards. But look ahead several boards as you near corners or end posts to adjust the gap slightly as needed.

Continued from pg. 33

8 *Recess two faces* on corner posts, and either lap the rails or take the time to miter the joint.

9 *Tie posts to the house* by counterboring and driving a lag screw long enough to reach into wall framing.

10 *Speed up picket installation* by leveling and installing corners, then filling in to string-line guides.

11 *Use a spacer* to keep the placement consistent. You can adjust several pickets slightly to fit final boards.

You can vary picket shape, spacing, and length to create a custom design and to incorporate a gate.

You can also vary rail sizes with a lighter rail on top and a larger rail to anchor the fence.

4

FENCE DESIGNS

Stepped Fences

A stepped fence generally has equally spaced posts but rails that step down the slope between them. It's one of the most basic ways to handle fences on sloping ground. To start with, you need to establish a level line across the slope, using stakes (the downhill being longer), string, and a line level.

You can mark off equal increments on the string and transfer the post locations to the ground with a plumb bob or level held against a straight 2x4.

The most attractive stepped fences have the same step height at the top between sections. To figure out the step height, first you must determine the overall height (rise) of the slope and divide that by the number of sections (the areas between the posts) to determine the size of the step. For example, if the total rise is 48 inches and the fence contains four equal sections, there should be 12-inch-high steps between posts.

It pays to lay out the steps on paper so you can see the length required for each post. In theory, you could cut the posts to length ahead of time. But that generally requires a lot of adjustments when you set them. Most people find it easier to set posts long, lay out the steps, and cut the posts as needed. Bear in mind that a stepped-fence layout is often a compromise. If the steps seem too large, you may have to use more posts, which allows each step to be shorter.

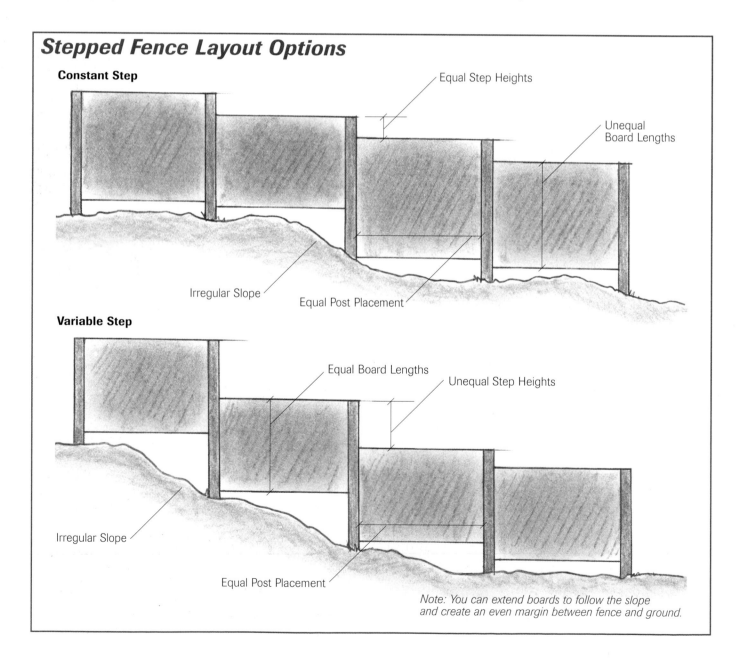

Stepped Fence Layout Options

Constant Step

Equal Step Heights

Unequal Board Lengths

Irregular Slope

Equal Post Placement

Variable Step

Equal Board Lengths

Unequal Step Heights

Irregular Slope

Equal Post Placement

Note: You can extend boards to follow the slope and create an even margin between fence and ground.

Stepped Fence Installation

TOOLS
- Shovel
- Circular saw
- Measuring tape
- Safety glasses
- Plumb bob
- Line level and 2' spirit level

MATERIALS
- Mason's twine
- Long 1x2s
- 2x4s for batter boards
- Concrete
- Spray paint

1 **Use a string and line level** to check the overall drop of the fence layout over the sloping ground.

2 **Measure the post locations** on the string, and use a plumb bob to transfer the locations to the ground.

3 **Set the posts** in their holes, and brace them in plumb position before backfilling or adding concrete.

4 **Use a level and straight 2x4** to mark the posts in a series of equal step-downs along the slope.

5 **Use a circular saw** to cut each post to it's correct step-down height. Be sure you have secure footing.

4

FENCE DESIGNS

Contour Fences

On a contoured fence, the rails run parallel with the slope without steps between posts. The fence follows the contour of the ground. These fences are easier to construct than stepped fences, especially on the uneven slopes of rolling terrain.

You lay out a contour fence the same way you lay out a basic straight fence. But you may need extra stakes to keep a hilly landscape from interfering with the layout lines. When installing posts for contoured fencing, set each post to the same height above the ground, and fasten each rail at the same height along each post so that they follow the contour of the slope.

Install picket boards so that they are plumb, rather than perpendicular to the rails. You can extend the boards several inches below the bottom rail and cut the ends to follow the contour of the ground.

Because sloping rails will be installed at different angles on contoured fence posts, they must be handled differently. The potential problem is most obvious if you make a plumb cut on the end of one rail along a flat section and try to join it with a plumb cut on a sloping rail. The sloped cut will be longer, sometimes significantly longer, creating a ragged, unfinished appearance.

The solution is to mark a cut through the overlapped boards. This splits the difference evenly and creates mating edges of equal size.

The posts are plumb but cut to different heights on a contour fence that follows the lay of the land.

Post and Rail Details

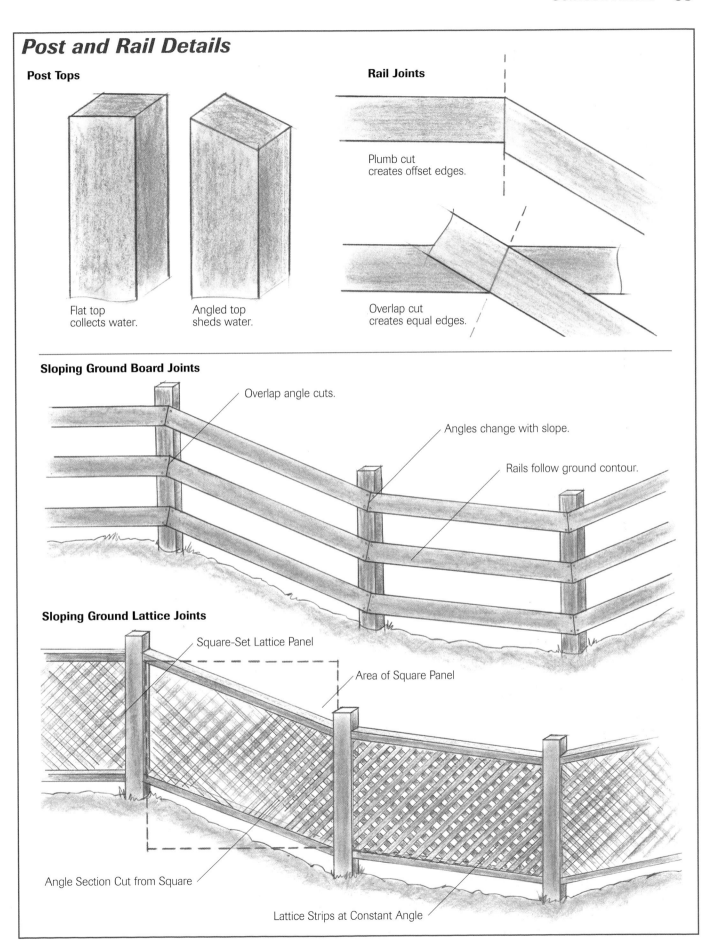

Post Tops

Flat top
collects water.

Angled top
sheds water.

Rail Joints

Plumb cut
creates offset edges.

Overlap cut
creates equal edges.

Sloping Ground Board Joints

Overlap angle cuts.

Angles change with slope.

Rails follow ground contour.

Sloping Ground Lattice Joints

Square-Set Lattice Panel

Area of Square Panel

Angle Section Cut from Square

Lattice Strips at Constant Angle

4

FENCE DESIGNS

Curved Fences

To build a curved fence, you must set the posts 48 to 72 inches on center along an arc. You can apply either straight or curved rails, depending on the look you are trying to create.

It takes curved rails to make a truly curved fence, but making curved rails is not as difficult as you might think. There are two basic ways to do it. One is to cut saw kerfs in the back of the rail so that it can bend without splitting or breaking. The other is to make the rail out of two separate pieces of 1x4 wood strung across several posts and screwed together to form a laminated rail. The rails must span at least three posts—rails won't form a curve if they span only two. Stagger the joints so that a joint on the top rail is not on the same post as a joint on a bottom rail.

With this approach it helps to soak the rails in water before use to make them more flexible. Attach the first piece to the posts with 3-inch galvanized deck screws, using two screws at each post. Then screw the second piece over the first, using 1¼-inch galvanized deck

screws, spaced about 8 inches apart. Stagger the screws so that one is near the top of the rail, the other near the bottom.

For tighter arcs, you can laminate thinner strips, called bender boards, or combine the two approaches by adding saw cuts about 1 inch apart to make the boards more flexible. Placing the kerfs on the inside of the curve will help shed water and prevent rot.

Curved fences often look best with narrow, lightweight boards, pickets, or slats attached vertically to the rails. Wide boards may split when attached to curved rails.

If the extra work of kerfing and laminating is too much on your project, consider a segmented fence. Instead of curved rails, you can attach short, straight fence sections to posts plotted along a curve.

This type of construction does not result in a smooth curve. Instead, you get a series of short straight runs that roughly follow an arc. You can smooth the angled edges by mitering the rail ends and the siding. Because the rails are straight, you can use wide boards or plywood for the siding.

Smart Tip ANGLE OPTION

Curves are difficult and time consuming to lay out accurately, and even more so to build. One efficient way around these drawbacks is to create a shallow angle at one post instead of a continuous curve over many posts. You can chamfer the post edges for better bearing or install connecting hardware. Boards can be spaced or mitered.

Curved fences can follow natural contours, including trees.

Cutting Saw-Kerf Curves

If you bend a one-by fence rail, the unnatural stress can cause splits and other problems. To relieve some of the stress and help the board bend, cut a series of half-deep saw-kerfs about every half inch on one face of the board (near right). You may want to use a square to help keep your cuts even. As you gradually bend the rail between posts and fasten pickets (far right), the kerfs close up. It's best if you can cover the kerfs with pickets.

Plotting a Smooth Curve

1. Find the corner by projecting both fence lines.

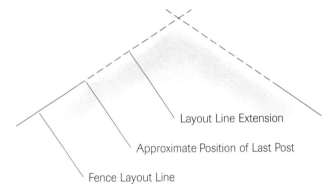

Layout Line Extension

Approximate Position of Last Post

Fence Layout Line

Note: Projected corner does not need to be 90 degrees.

2. Measure from corner to tangent points of curve.

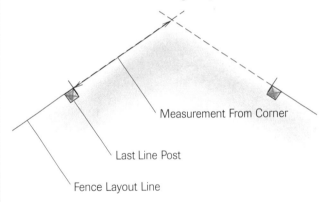

Measurement From Corner

Last Line Post

Fence Layout Line

Note: Larger distances from corner produce larger arcs.

3. Construct lines perpendicular to the fence line.

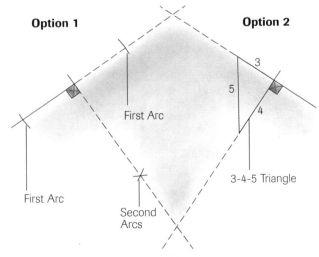

Option 1

Option 2

First Arc

First Arc

Second Arcs

3
5
4

3-4-5 Triangle

4. Swing curve from intersection of perpendicular lines.

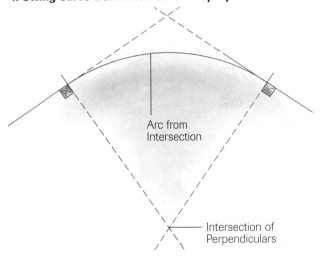

Arc from Intersection

Intersection of Perpendiculars

*Note: **Option 1:** Swing equal arcs to each side of the post, and swing a new arc from each mark. The point where those arcs intersect is perpendicular to the post. **Option 2:** You can instead use 3-4-5 triangulation.*

Fence Posts

Posts anchor the structure of a fence and contribute to the overall design.

Setting Posts

The first step in building a fence is marking the fence location with stakes and string. Once you've done that, mark post locations along the string with tape, bright-colored chalk, or spray paint. If you're installing the fence on a property line or if the fence must meet certain setback requirements, you'll need to establish the exact location of the line to avoid disputes with neighbors or to make sure the fence meets local ordinances. Once you locate your property lines, mark the corners with surveyor's stakes or other markers.

If you're building a fence within the property, first you'll need to establish the locations of the end posts and corner posts. This is usually done by measuring out from one or more existing reference points, such as the house, the driveway, an existing fence, or other landmarks. If you haven't already done so, draw up a site plan for your project.

In most cases, you can find reliable reference in your own records of the house and property. If you have ever built an addition or made major improvements requiring a building permit, chances are that you needed drawings, including a measured site plan.

You also can find reference in the form of a survey, which is generally part of any house sale. Another resource is the town clerk. In many areas there is a record of your property that includes the location,

Post Installation

TOOLS

- Posthole digger
- Measuring tape
- Shovel
- Level
- Drill-driver
- Hoe
- Trowel
- Hammer

MATERIALS

- Stakes
- String
- Braces
- Concrete
- Posts
- Gravel
- Spray paint

1 **Square up your layout,** string lines to stakes set outside the work area, and mark the corner posts.

2 **Mark the ground** with paint or chalk so that you can remove the lines to dig postholes.

3 **In soft soil** you can use a posthole digger. For digging many holes, consider renting a power auger.

Continued on pg. 46

general size, and placement of buildings on the site.

After plotting the fence line, you can mark the post locations on the ground, dig the postholes, and install the posts. Once the posts are set, you'll add the rails and siding for the particular design you've chosen. If your design calls for you to notch, or dado, the posts, it's easier to do this before setting them. If you haven't chosen a design yet, thumb through the wood fence projects in Chapter 6, pages 60 to 69.

As a rule of thumb, fence posts are set with about one-third of their total length in the ground and at a minimum of 24 inches deep. In areas subject to frost heave, it is recommended that you set the bottoms of the posts at least 6 inches below the frost line to avoid heaving. Average frost-depth tables are available from your local building department. It's always good practice to check local building codes and standard practices in your particular area.

The one-third rule applies especially to gate, end, corner, and any posts that support heavy siding material. Solid-board or panel fences exposed to high winds may also require deeper posts. However, the rule does not always make the best use of standard precut lumber lengths—a 72-inch-high fence would require a 9-foot post, for example. For this reason, most 72-inch fences can use 96-inch posts sunk 24 inches into the ground. But the end posts, corner posts, and gate posts on such a fence should be the full 9 feet long.

Continued from pg. 45

4 **Check the depth** *to keep the holes consistent. Digging below the average frost depth will prevent heaving.*

5 **Add some gravel** *to promote drainage and firm up a base for the post and supporting concrete.*

8 **Mix concrete** *from bags in a portable tub for only a few posts. Consider renting a power mixer on large jobs.*

9 **Shovel the concrete** *into the hole. Try not to dislodge dirt around the post; it can weaken the mix.*

Decorative posts can define an entry and provide extra strength to support a gate.

6 **Set the post** *(cut slightly long for final trimming in most cases), and check it for plumb.*

7 **Fasten braces** *at right angles to secure the post. If working alone, use clamps as you adjust for plumb.*

10 **Use a shovel handle** *to eliminate air pockets and work the concrete completely around the post.*

11 **Encourage drainage** *away from the post by mounding up some concrete a few inches above grade.*

Post Foundations

Posts are typically set in tamped earth, tamped gravel, or concrete and gravel. But there are many ways to provide support, such as setting a flat stone 4 to 6 inches thick as a footing.

Whether or not you decide to use concrete depends largely on the fence design and soil conditions. Generally, you can use earth-and-gravel fill if the soil is not too loose, sandy, or subject to shifting or frost heaves, and if the fence posts don't have to support much weight. Post-and-board fences, lattice, spaced pickets, or fences less than 60 inches tall are all light enough for earth-and-gravel fill. In extremely loose or sandy soils you can attach 1x4 pressure-treated cleats to the bottoms of the posts to provide lateral stability.

Using Concrete

For added stability, use concrete, especially in areas with deep frost lines. You can even drive 16d nails partially into the post before placing the concrete to lock the post and concrete together.

If precise post spacing is required (such as when dadoing or mortising rails into posts or attaching prefabricated fence panels or sections), you'll need to set the posts successively, fitting in rails or sections as you set each post. Use fast-setting concrete mixes for this type of construction.

There are many ways to set posts in holes. You can pour concrete around the post, plumb and brace it, and attach the rails or panels when the concrete hardens. Many contractors use this approach, but for most do-it-yourselfers it pays to plumb and brace each post securely before pouring concrete. This system keeps you from disrupting the mix (or dislodging dirt) as you add and adjust the braces. As you fill in successive sections between posts, occasionally recheck the entire fence for plumb.

If you don't use concrete to secure the posts, it's important to compact the backfill you do use, even if it's gravel. The best approach is to add fill-in layers 6 to 12 inches thick. Use a 2x4, or better yet a 4x4 if you can heft one, to pack down material. This step solidifies the fill around the post.

If you're not sure of local building practices, seek advice from the building department or ask several local fence contractors for recommended practices suited to the ground in your area.

Backfill Options

Fence posts normally are set in one of the four basic ways shown below. Posts deeply embedded in solid, compacted soil may not need a foundation stone if they carry a lightweight fence. But corner posts and posts that support heavy gates, trellises, or other additional structures need the most secure installation.

Earth

Gravel

Gravel and Cleats

Concrete and Gravel

Beefy posts on a delicate looking fence can carry the weight of entry and driveway gates.

Notching Posts

Most fences are built with rails or panels nailed to the surfaces of the supporting posts. But on some fences, particularly designs with only a few widely spaced rails, you may want to dress up the installation by recessing the horizontal boards into the posts.

The best tool for cutting these recesses, called dadoes, is a table saw because it's easy to make accurate repetitive cuts. But on most fence projects the posts are too long to maneuver in a shop, and you have to use a circular saw.

Start by laying out the borders of the recess. Then set the saw blade to equal the depth of the recess.

Carefully make two clean cuts (using a square as a guide will help) along your marks. Then make several passes to create saw kerfs between the two edge cuts.

You don't have to make dozens of cuts, each one no wider than the thickness of the saw blade. Instead, make cuts that leave thin shafts of wood in place. The more cuts you make, the thinner the shafts will be and the easier they will be to remove.

When you're done cutting, knock down the shafts with a hammer. This will clear away most of the wood, but leave rough ends on several of the shafts. Clear them away using a hammer and chisel to make sure that the bottom of the dado is flat. You can also recess two-by boards to only half of their thickness.

Notching a Post

TOOLS
- Circular saw (with square guide)
- Hammer
- Chisel
- Combination square and pencil
- Sawhorses
- Line level
- Measuring tape
- Safety glasses

MATERIALS
- Posts
- String

1 **To notch posts for rails,** carefully make square cuts equal to depth (or half the depth) of the rails.

3 **Multiple kerfs** weaken the wood, and allow you to break out the notch area with a hammer.

4 **Clean the floor of the notch** with a hammer and chisel to allow the fence rail to seat cleanly.

A fence with widely spaced pickets can define a yard or garden without closing it off from other areas.

2 **Make the edge cuts first,** *using a square guide. Then cut multiple kerfs about ½ in. apart between them.*

5 **Cut notches on a bench,** *and align the poles. Another option is to make the cuts on installed poles.*

FANCY-CUT POSTS

If you want to create a decorative detail on the tops of the posts, you can make a bevel cut along the edges with a circular saw. Make a small cut along the very edge (or trim each edge with a plane), or make a deeper cut that creates a wider bevel. In theory, you can make four deep cuts that turn the top of the post into a pyramid shape. But partial chamfers generally look better. Any slope, even a simple angle cut, helps to shed water and preserve the end grain of the post.

5

FENCE POSTS

Decorative Posts

You may want to make one or more cuts on all the fence posts to help them shed water. But on most fence projects only a few key posts are candidates for trim, caps, and other decorative details.

There are many types of preformed caps that you can screw or nail onto posts beside a gate, for example. Most are made of wood with some type of slope to help shed water. Some are covered with folded copper sheeting, while others have molded edges to create the look of molding.

You can also find highly decorative pieces, called finials, that screw into the top of a post. The most basic are simply rounded shapes. More complex finial shapes range from urns to pineapples and other exotic and sculptural objects.

Another option, if you're only dealing with a few posts, is to build up the decorative details yourself. The general approach is to select a series of complementary molding profiles that you can add around the post. To make more of an impact you can also clad the post top with one-by lumber before trimming.

Once you have selected the moldings, make a series of level marks around all four sides of the post as a guide. Then cut miters on the molding, and attach each piece with exterior-grade glue and finishing nails. You may want to predrill narrow moldings.

Decorative Post Caps and Finials

Brass Federal

Classic

Copper Hightop

Plateau

Federal

Ball

Royal

Acorn

Finishing Posts

TOOLS
- Hammer
- Paint brush
- Router (optional)
- Saw
- Combination square

MATERIALS
- Molding
- Stain, sealer, or paint
- Threaded finial
- Exterior-grade glue
- Finishing nails

1 *Miter the corners* on strips of trim, and set them near the top of the post with exterior glue and finishing nails.

Build up decorative posts with one-by lumber, multiple layers of mitered trim, and a carved finial as a finishing touch.

2 **Add a decorative top cap** to the post (perhaps making your own with a router), and screw on a finial.

3 **Protect the wood** with two coats of clear sealer, semi-transparent or solid-body stain, or paint.

5

FENCE POSTS

Obstructions

If you find obstacles such as trees, boulders, or drainage areas interfering with your fence line, you can remove the obstacle, move the fence line, or build the fence to skirt or incorporate the obstacle. The last choice is normally the most practical.

If a tree stands in your fence line, set the posts as close as possible to the tree, but avoid damaging its roots. Install the fence rails and then the siding so that they extend beyond the posts toward the tree. To keep these sections from sagging, use hardware to reinforce the post connections, and install diagonal braces made from siding material.

Where a fence crosses a low area, extend boards below the bottom rail to follow the contour. Do not extend boards farther than about 8 inches below the bottom rail or the ends will tend to warp.

If the fence must cross a swale, ditch, or small stream that contains water during the rainy season, construct a grate from lengths of No. 3 rebar or ½-inch galvanized pipe, spaced about 6 inches apart. The grate will keep people and large animals from crawling underneath the fence. Drill holes through a bottom rail made from a 2x4. Attach the rail to the fence, insert pipe or rebar through each hole, and drive the bars into the ground. As an extra measure, you can set the grate into a ribbon of concrete.

Building up to Obstructions

TOOLS
- Drill-driver
- Circular saw
- String or chalk-line box
- Measuring tape
- Sliding T-bevel
- Safety glasses

MATERIALS
- Posts
- Post hardware
- Panel sections
- Brace
- Nails or screws

1 *Set the last post* as close as possible to the obstruction, and measure the rise required in the bottom rail.

2 *Build the last panel section* with the angled rail, and cut off the boards following the same angle.

3 *Support the last panel* on post hardware, and screw on a diagonal brace to keep the bottom rail from sagging.

Extended rails and partial pickets join this property-line tree.

You can also add an extra support post adjacent to trees.

Extending a Fence

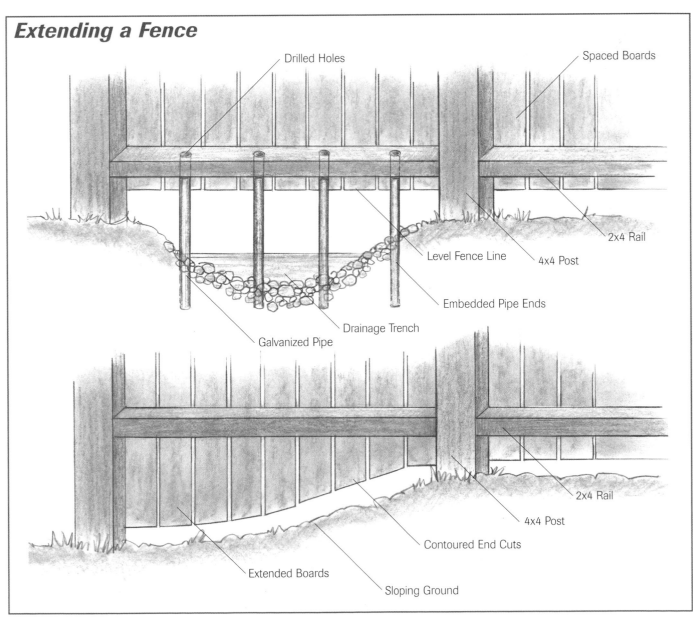

Drilled Holes

Spaced Boards

Level Fence Line

2x4 Rail

4x4 Post

Embedded Pipe Ends

Drainage Trench

Galvanized Pipe

2x4 Rail

4x4 Post

Contoured End Cuts

Extended Boards

Sloping Ground

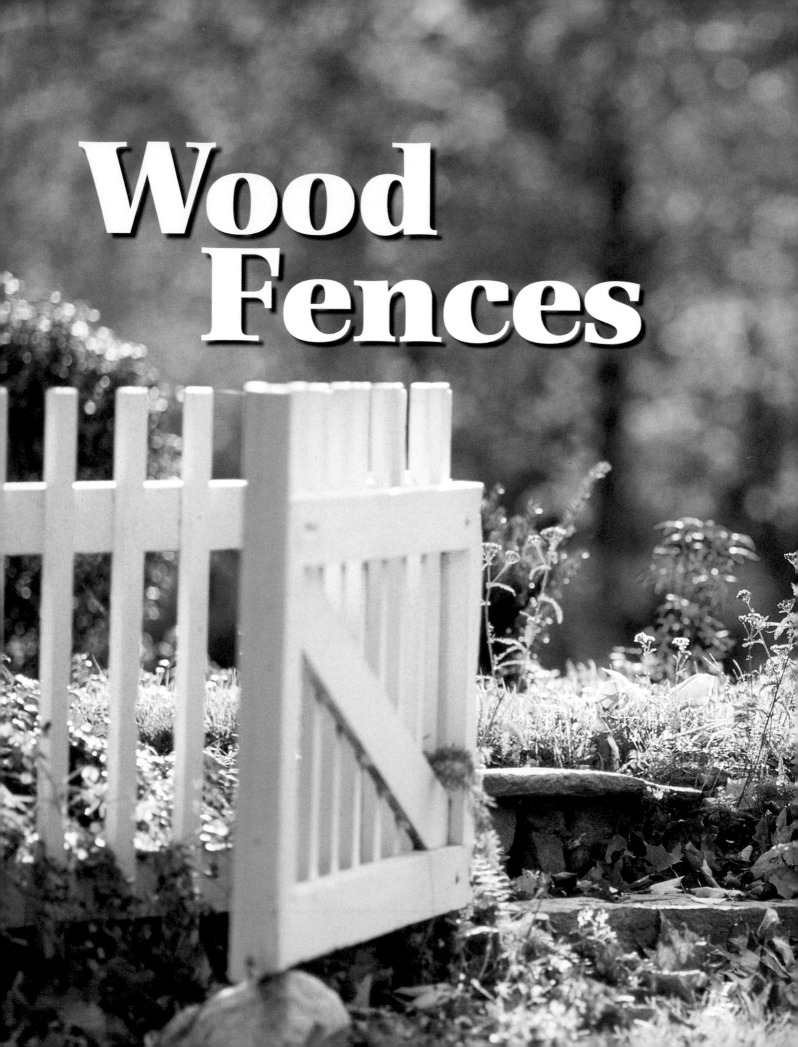

Wood
Fences

Picket Fence Styles

Picket fences are often found gracing the front yards of colonial, Victorian, and other traditionally styled houses, although pickets are appropriate for almost any house. As opposed to solid-board fences, the open design of a picket fence shows off plantings within the yard yet provides a definite boundary. Planting low shrubs, vines, or perennials next to the fence helps soften the design.

Some lumberyards and home centers carry precut pickets, but the designs are often limited. To make your own, clamp two or three boards together and cut the tops with a handsaw or circular saw. To make fancier shapes, cut the pattern with a saber saw.

Most picket fences are 36 to 48 inches tall, supported on a framework of 4x4 posts with 2x4 rails. Posts generally extend above the picket tops, and have some type of decorative top. But you can also run the top rail along the tops of the posts and let the pickets rise above the rail.

The pickets themselves usually consist of evenly spaced 1x3s or 1x4s attached to the outside of the rails. You can increase or decrease the spacing depending on the amount of privacy you want. It's smart to keep the bottoms of the pickets at least 2 inches above the ground to prevent decay and make it easier both to paint the fence and to remove weeds.

Picket Styles

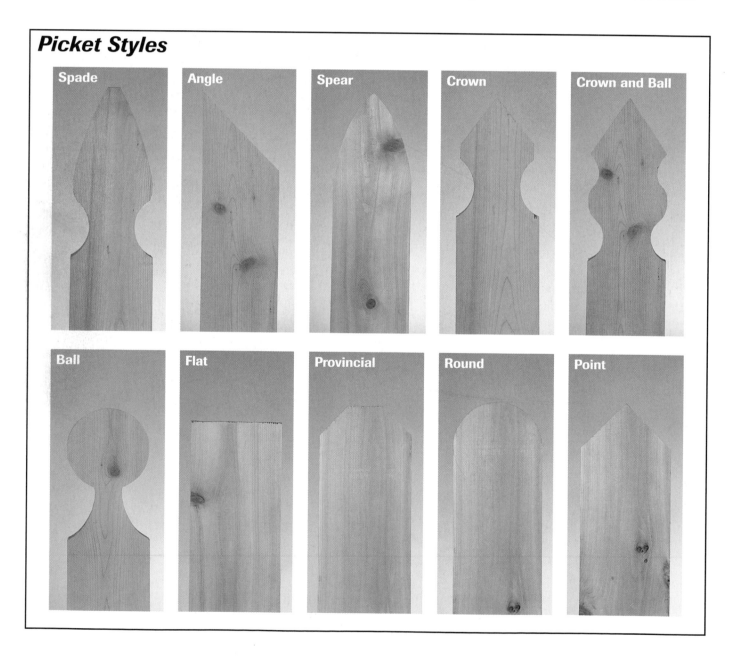

Spade · Angle · Spear · Crown · Crown and Ball

Ball · Flat · Provincial · Round · Point

Rail Connectors

Nailed Butt Joint

Nailed On Edge

Screwed Hardware

Recessed

You can create a custom picket shape with various edge cuts and use one master as a template to cut others.

Basic Picket Fence

There are many ways to build a frame for a basic picket fence. One of the most practical is to install the lower rail between posts and the upper rail on top of the posts. By using long lengths of lumber for the top rail, you can connect three or more posts, which makes the overall structure strong. Join upper rails at the centerline of a post, predrilling to avoid splits where you must nail close to the ends.

Spacing your pickets is often a compromise and depends to some extent on the width of the pickets. If you use pickets as wide as the posts, it looks best to have a full picket covering each post. It requires a lot of planning to have equal picket spacing on a long fence work out this well, though. One option is to use an oversize, more decorative picket over the post and smaller, plainer pickets between them.

One of the nice parts of building a picket fence, however, is that you can make small adjustments among many pickets to take up the slack in a layout that isn't exact. If the posts are only a few feet apart, spacing is more difficult. The narrower the pickets (on any post layout) the more room there is for adjustment. The traditional approach is to use the thickness of the picket as a spacer. But you can cut a spacer stick to the size you need. Always clamp or tack a series in place to be sure of the spacing.

Post Top Variations

There are many ways to top posts aside from a basic square cut. Some of the best options combine decorative detail with the ability to shed water, which can shorten post life by causing rot where it collects on the porous end grain. The easiest approach is to make an angled cut. Chamfering the top edges also helps. Adding a full cap rail, either chamfered or angled, also reinforces the fence.

Angle Cut

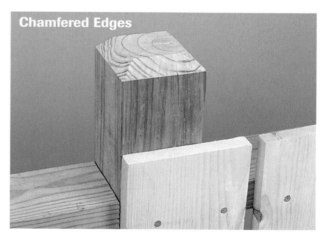

Chamfered Edges

Flat Cap with Chamfers

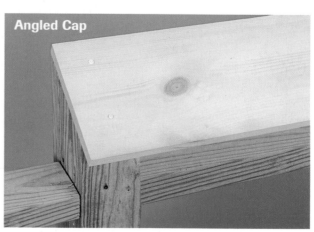

Angled Cap

Picket Fence Basics

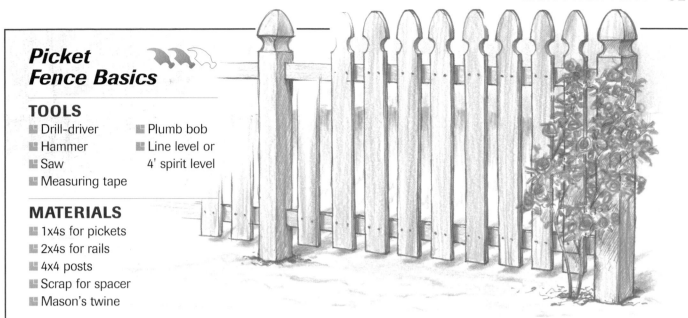

TOOLS
- Drill-driver
- Hammer
- Saw
- Measuring tape
- Plumb bob
- Line level or 4' spirit level

MATERIALS
- 1x4s for pickets
- 2x4s for rails
- 4x4 posts
- Scrap for spacer
- Mason's twine

1 **When notching posts, leveling, and fastening rails** it helps to clamp the rail in position as you work.

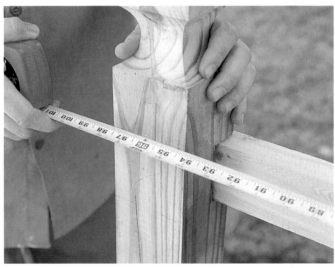

2 **To figure picket layout,** measure between end posts and divide by picket width plus picket spacing.

3 **Use taut string lines** and a line level to guide picket installation over long lengths of horizontal rail.

4 **Instead of measuring,** use a spacer stick to maintain picket layout. Double-check periodically with a level.

6

WOOD FENCES

Vertical-Board Fence

Once you establish a basic box frame of posts and rails, you can install vertical boards in a variety of configurations. To increase privacy and wind protection, for example, you can use tongue-and-groove planks to form a solid barrier. Or you can use wide boards with equally wide spaces to create a partial screen and lattice-like support for climbing plants.

One of the most popular variations is a two-sided board design built around 4x4 posts connected by 2x4 rails. You can use smooth or rough-sawn boards of different sizes to cover the frame, but 1x6s generally have enough strength to span between rails even on a high fence. (Remember that many regions have codes that restrict fence height.) Once the posts are set, use a string and line level to mark the locations of U-shaped galvanized hardware. Nail the hardware to the insides of the posts, and the rails to the hardware.

Plumb the first board, and use a scrap piece to lay out spaces between boards. Then create an offset version of the same layout on the other side of the rails.

The overall effect is a combination of solid protection and privacy that is lighter and airier than a solid wood fence. And unlike many fence designs, this offset plan creates a fence that looks the same on both sides, which can be an asset if your fence plans have an impact on a neighbor.

Oversized, capped corner posts contrast with delicate pickets.

Lattice alone or with boards (pages 64 to 65) can be attractive.

Sturdy vertical-board fencing supports climbing vines.

Vertical Fence Basics

TOOLS
- Hammer
- Shovel
- Drill
- Measuring tape
- Saw
- Pencil
- Safety glasses

MATERIALS
- 2x4s for rails
- 1x6 boards for siding
- 6d galvanized nails
- Galvanized rail hardware and nails

1 **Establish the fence frame** by fastening galvanized framing hardware on the inside of the posts.

2 **Set the rails on the brackets,** level the rails, and drive nails through the flanges to secure the rails.

3 **Use a scrap** board to lay out the staggered pattern of one board and one space on each side of the rails.

4 **You can nail alternate sides** as you go or set boards on one side until complete and then add more to the other side.

Lattice-and-Board Fence

Lattice-and-board fences are an attractive and versatile combination of two basic fence types: a solid-board fence for maximum privacy and shelter, and a see-through lattice panel on top that provides a decorative touch and an airy appearance. You can adjust the proportions, of course, using shorter boards and longer lattice panels, as desired. The combination offers good wind protection near a patio or deck, while retaining an open feeling.

Framing Lattice

You can fabricate your own lattice panels to achieve the spacing and angle you want. But there are many stock lattice configurations available, including basic squares and diamonds in plain wood, pressure-treated wood, and vinyl. Vinyl lattice is generally colored. It doesn't make a good match with naturally finished wood but does blend in if you paint or stain the fence.

For most of these fences you can build a stock assembly of posts and rails with two additions. One is a subrail that divides the board section from the lattice section. The other is an interior frame of small nailer strips that supports and captures both the edges of the lattice panel and the ends of the boards.

Once you build the basic frame, you need to add nailers inside it. The nailers support both the board and lattice but also serve to trim the panels. One option is to install only one set of nailers and nail the lower boards and upper lattice against them. For a more finished look, make a duplicate set to cover the edges of both fence sections. The best approach is to rip nailers from extra fence board material, creating 1x1 strips.

If you buy lattice panels, you'll need to cut them to fit. Use an old saw blade and wear eye protection during this operation because your saw is bound to hit a few staples that hold together the lattice panels. You can simply set the lattice in place before securing it with the trim strips set with finishing nails.

The bottom portion of the fence can be made from interlocking tongue-and-groove boards, basic slats with a space between them, or a combination of boards and covering battens,

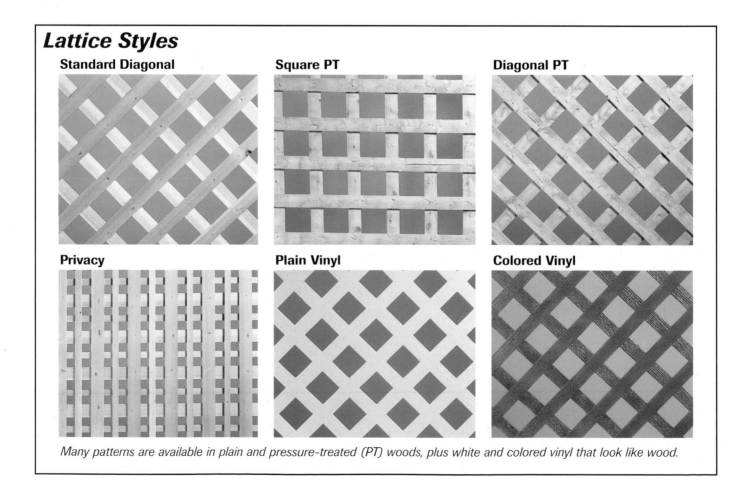

Lattice Styles

Standard Diagonal   **Square PT**   **Diagonal PT**

Privacy   **Plain Vinyl**   **Colored Vinyl**

Many patterns are available in plain and pressure-treated (PT) woods, plus white and colored vinyl that look like wood.

Lattice Fence Basics

TOOLS
- Drill
- Hammer
- Spirit level
- Saw
- Measuring tape

MATERIALS
- 1x1 nailer strip
- 4x4 posts
- 2x4 rails
- Lattice panel
- T&G boards
- Nails

1 **The keys to a fence** with both board and lattice panels are nailer strips attached to the horizontal rails.

2 **Nail vertical tongue-and-groove boards** against the nailing strips on the bottom and mid-height rails.

3 **Set your precut lattice panel** against nailers fastened on both the mid-height and upper rails.

4 **Add a second nailer** on the opposite side of the fence as trim to conceal the cut ends of the lattice.

Rustic Fence

This fence has rustic charm and works well on uneven terrain. It defines space without blocking a view and allows you to cover a lot of ground with minimal effort and materials.

Rails are available at many lumberyards and garden centers. They may be square or roughly wedge-shaped and are typically 72 to 96 inches long. Some outlets carry premortised posts and pretenoned rails. To use them, just make sure that your post layout is correct and allows for the tenon overlaps. But you can also buy rough rail stock and shape the parts yourself.

Start by making tapered cuts 8 to 10 inches long on the ends of the rails. Two tapered rails together should form a narrow center section where rails overlap inside the posts. Precise cuts are not required with this style of fence, but you should make the tapers approximately the same size. The same goes for the post mortises. Another approach is to use pressure-treated 2x4s with a standard half-lap joint that is concealed inside the mortise.

Once you determine the combined width of overlapped rails, make the post mortises just slightly wider. The easiest method is to drill out the mortise with a wide bit, although you can use a smaller bit and make more holes. Finish by trimming the inside edges with a hammer and chisel.

Rustic Fence Basics

TOOLS
- Drill
- Hammer
- Shovel
- 4' spirit level
- Wood chisel
- Measuring tape
- Safety glasses
- Saw

MATERIALS
- Posts and rails
- 2x4 braces
- 1x2 stakes
- Concrete mix
- 8d galvanized nails

3 **Set the post,** and adjust the footing and backfill as needed for the mortises to line up post to post.

4 **Check the posts for plumb** and attach one or more temporary braces to secure them.

Alternate Rustic Rails

Rustic-style post-and-rail fences are generally available with posts already notched and rails already tapered. But you can also use rough lumber and make those cuts yourself. Another low-cost option is to use 2x4s for the rails in place of stock rails with tapered ends. Instead of making a typical side-by-side rustic joint, simply cut a half-lap so that the boards join inside the post notch. With the 2x4s on edge, the lap itself is concealed inside the post. Pressure-treated 2x4s are the best choice for economy rails. But you may want to apply two coats of preservative and penetrating stain in any case to get a color match between the posts and rails.

1 **To mortise through your own posts,** mark the area and drill through from both sides to clear the wood.

2 **Clean up the outer edges and insides** of the mortise with a hammer and sharp chisel.

5 **Stock rails are tapered** so that they overlap through the mortise. Nails secure both rails at the same time.

6 **When the rails are installed** you can recheck for plumb and complete the backfilling.

6

WOOD FENCES

Horizontal-Board Fence

A typical horizontal-board fence has a classic, almost formal appearance that's well suited to contemporary home designs. It is most practical on flat ground, although you can adjust for changes in terrain by creating matching angle cuts over posts.

The basic design uses a framework of 4x4 posts set 8 feet on center and two or more rows of 1x6 rails. You can dramatically alter the appearance and function of this basic fence by using three or four horizontal rails, among other options. If need be you can add a 1x6 vertical board nailed midspan between posts to reinforce the horizontal rails and minimize bowing.

Among other options, you can use a combination of different board widths to make a repeating pattern, or a wide board near the ground and progressively narrower boards above.

You can also add a cap rail over the posts of a board fence. The best type of cap has a slight slope, which means you need to cut the post tops ahead of time. Without the angle cuts, the nails holding the cap can work loose over time, allowing the wood to cup. This tends to trap water and lead to rot.

When you install the rails (and a cap), be sure to stagger joints on a long run. You can use rough-sawn lumber or even siding boards to match your house. But stagger joints on different posts.

Alternate Horizontal Board Styles

The most economical pattern, and the easiest to install, is the basic four-board fence (below). For more protection you can add a mid-board or several boards with small spaces between them. Another twist on this idea is to use different widths to create a pattern (right). But even keeping the pattern simple, alternating wide and narrow boards can sometimes create an overly busy look. Another classic board-fence pattern is the basic X-shape between posts, used in combination with top and bottom rails.

Patterned Board

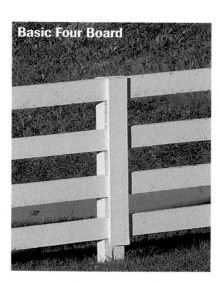
Basic Four Board

Cross Board

Horizontal Fence Basics

TOOLS
- Hammer
- Drill
- Saw
- Line level
- Measuring tape
- Safety glasses

MATERIALS
- Mason's twine
- 1x6 rails
- 4x4 posts
- 2" galvanized screws

1 ***You can notch posts ahead of time*** *and adjust them to a level string as you set them in the ground.*

2 ***The easiest way*** *to level a string is with a line level. It has a bubble vial and hooks onto a taut line.*

3 ***Reduce the chance of splitting boards*** *by predrilling where rails butt over a post.*

4 ***Join horizontal rails*** *at the center of a post. Stagger joints in upper and lower rails on different posts.*

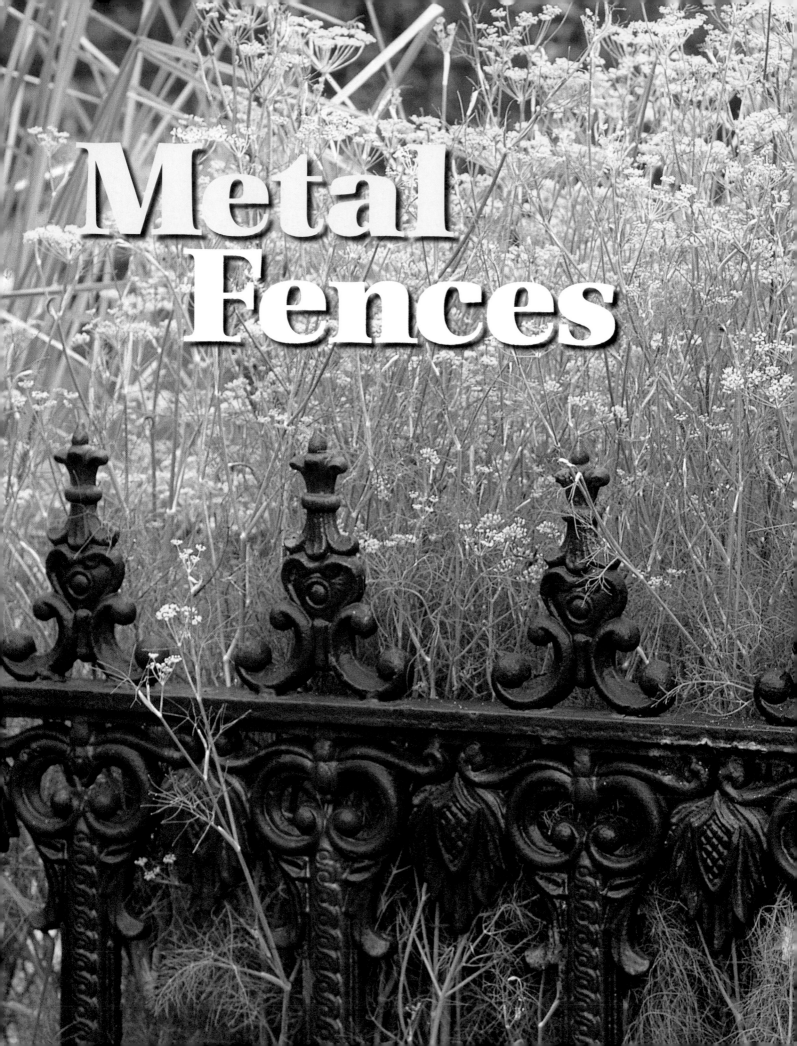

Metal
Fences

Chain-Link Fences

Many people think of wood pickets and boards when they think of a fence. But most buyers choose utilitarian chain-link fencing because it's strong, durable, and inexpensive compared with many wood styles. In fact, the country's largest fence manufacturer sells more chain-link fencing than any other type, and says that it is number one among the many types and styles in the $2.3 billion fence market.

A low chain-link fence is relatively easy to install. (For a tall fence, it's wise to hire a qualified fence contractor.) Even though the components are metal, you follow the basic procedures for measuring and laying out the job, excavating the holes, and setting the posts. But bear in mind that chain-link systems (the rails in particular) are not as adjustable as wooden boards that you can quickly trim to fit. It's important to have your layout dead-on and the posts plumb.

Overall, chain-link fences consists of simple fit-together parts. You assemble them almost like plumbing pipes, fitting rails to posts with connectors and creating a frame on which you fasten the chain link.

Granted, this is not the most elegant style of fence. But on the plus side, chain link does not require painting and doesn't warp, rot, or become food for termites. And you can weave plastic strips through the links to increase privacy and add some color. (See page 77.)

Chain-Link Connectors

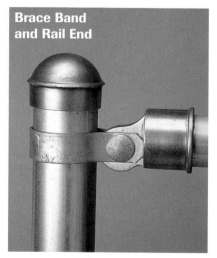

Brace Band and Rail End

Connects the rail to the post.

Loop-Top Holder, Intermediate Post

Caps intermediate post with holder.

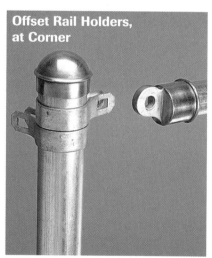

Offset Rail Holders, at Corner

Allows connectors to level rails.

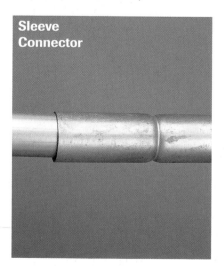

Sleeve Connector

Joins rail sections on long runs.

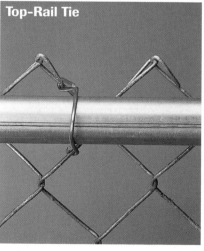

Top-Rail Tie

Secures the top row of closed links.

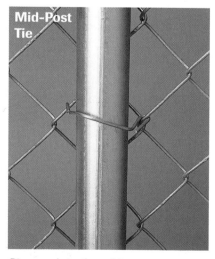

Mid-Post Tie

Pins mesh to the mid-post support.

Chain-Link Fence Parts

GATE LATCHES

Fork Latch

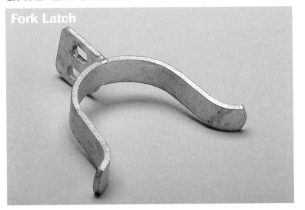

Butterfly Swing-Through Latch

GATE HINGES

Post-Mount Pin Hinge

Gate-Mount Hinge

POST PARTS

Post-Mount Brace Band

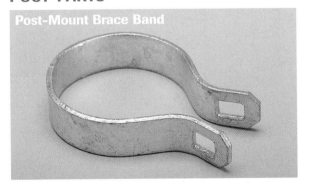

End and Top Caps

HARDWARE

Hog Rings

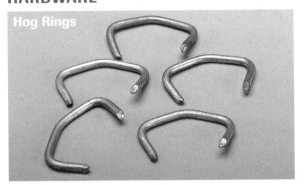

Nuts and Bolts

Installation Options

Chain-link mesh is galvanized with zinc or aluminum coated for a more durable finish. You can also buy vinyl-coated chain-link mesh, usually in white, black, brown, or green. Dark colors often allow the fence to blend into the surroundings, particularly if you purchase matching vinyl sleeves to cover the tubular metal posts and rails.

Galvanized mesh is usually the least expensive, but durability and price depend on the quality of the galvanized coating. Vinyl-coated chain-link mesh is the most expensive, but it offers more design choices and generally outlasts galvanized or aluminum mesh. Aluminum mesh is generally better than galvanized because it looks nicer and lasts a bit longer. You need to plan the fence project and assemble the many components. The biggest challenge may be tracking down a fence puller—the tool that stretches the chain-link mesh between the posts. A fence puller (generally used with a come-along), consists of a fence-pulling bar and hooks that grip the chain links. You may have to check several tool rental shops before you find one that carries fence pullers.

When you set the posts in concrete, bear in mind that terminal posts (end, corner, and gate posts) often have larger diameters, and are set about 3 inches higher than intermediate posts. Use a fairly stiff mix, and check to make sure that the posts are plumb.

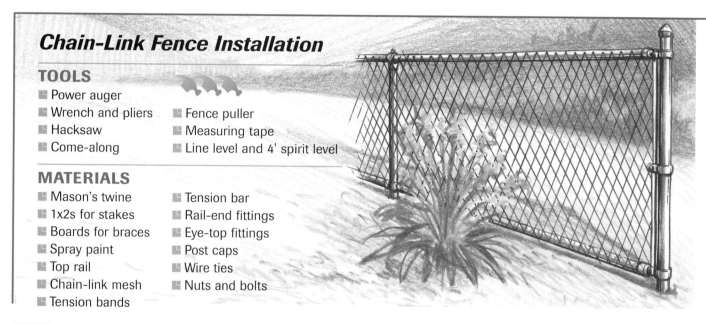

Chain-Link Fence Installation

TOOLS

- Power auger
- Wrench and pliers
- Hacksaw
- Come-along
- Fence puller
- Measuring tape
- Line level and 4' spirit level

MATERIALS

- Mason's twine
- 1x2s for stakes
- Boards for braces
- Spray paint
- Top rail
- Chain-link mesh
- Tension bands
- Tension bar
- Rail-end fittings
- Eye-top fittings
- Post caps
- Wire ties
- Nuts and bolts

3 **Brace terminal posts securely in two directions,** and string a level line to locate intermediate posts.

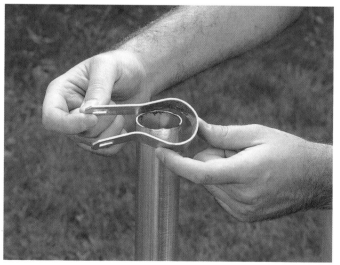

4 **Slide several tension bands** over each terminal post. These clip into the tension bar and fasten it to the post.

Stretching Chain-Link

You can roll out chain-link mesh and pull it reasonably taut by hand. But to remove final ripples you need some mechanical advantage. Apply it by hooking one end of a come-along to a bracket on a terminal post (right). You can brace the post if you're pulling a lot of mesh. Attach the other end to a pulling rod woven through the links of the fencing (far right). Crank the come-along to take up any slack before fastening the loose end of mesh to the next pole.

1 **Check the staked layout strings** for square, and mark the post locations with spray paint or chalk.

2 **On most jobs,** it pays to rent a gasoline-powered auger. This one is a handful, even for two people.

5 **Bolt brace bands** with rail-end fittings to the terminal posts. The lower edge of mesh often is braced with wire.

6 **Set loop-top fittings** onto intermediate posts, and slide the top rail through them to reach the terminal posts.

7

METAL FENCES

Continued on pg. 76

Adding Rails and Mesh

Set the terminal posts first. The line posts are usually several inches lower and capped with eye-fittings that secure the upper rails. When the post concrete hardens (in one or two days) fit three or four tension bands (depending on fence height) on each terminal post, along with a brace band to anchor the top rail, and a terminal post cap.

Gently tap the eye tops into the ends of the line posts using a hammer and a block of wood. Bolt the rail ends onto the brace bands on the terminal posts, and then install the top rails, slipping them through the eye-top connectors on the line posts and into the rail ends. Often, one end of each rail is reduced in diameter so that you can fit the end snugly into the rail preceding it. In other cases, you may need sleeves to connect rail ends. Rail-to-rail connections do not have to occur exactly above a post, although the installation will be stronger if they do.

With a helper, unroll several feet of chain-link mesh, and weave a tension bar into the end of the mesh. Attach the bar to the tension bands on the end or corner post using the carriage bolts provided. Pull the mesh tightly by hand, and weave a fence-pulling rod into the mesh about 36 inches in front of the end post. Hook one end of a come-along to the pulling rod and the other end to the end post. Then crank the come-along to tighten the mesh and apply fasteners.

Continued from pg. 75

7 *Slide the top rail* into one of the rail-end fittings bolted to a terminal post with brace bands.

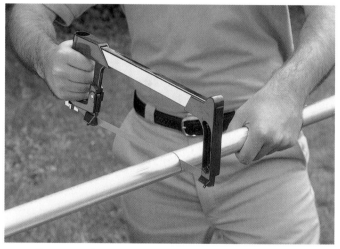

8 *On many fence layouts* you will need to cut the rails to fit with a hacksaw. It's best to splice rails at a post.

11 *Space tension bands* on the post (generally three for a low fence), and bolt them to the tension bar.

12 *You can tighten the mesh* with a special pulling bar by hand, or use a pulling rod with a come-along.

Disguising a Chain-Link Fence

Chain-link fencing is certainly not the most attractive fence you can install. It may be the most durable and among the strongest, but it can't blend in with your house or yard the way a wood fence can. However, most fence suppliers carry colored plastic strips that you can use to put a more palatable face on the mesh. To install them, simply weave the strips through the mesh. You can install them vertically (right) or diagonally (far right) to help the fence blend in.

9 **Some rails have a reduced diameter** on one end (top). For same-size ends, use a sleeve connector (bottom).

10 **Roll out the fencing,** and weave a tension bar in and out through the mesh links near the terminal post.

13 **Link the mesh to the top rail** with galvanized wire, or use S-shaped ties available from chain-link suppliers.

14 **Once the mesh is taut and secured,** you can finish the project by fitting on posts caps.

Wood-and-Wire Fences

Welded- or woven-wire mesh on a wood frame makes a lightweight, economical, easy-to-build fence that's a good choice for enclosing play areas for children or defining garden areas. Extend the posts, and this design serves well as a trellis for climbing vines.

Welded wire comes in a variety of gauges and mesh sizes, typically in 36-, 48-, and 72-inch widths, in 50- or 100-foot rolls. Choose the heaviest-gauge wire available, as thin wire can easily deform and is prone to rust. Most wood-and-wire fences have a 2 x 2- or 2 x 4-inch galvanized or vinyl-coated grid. Vinyl-coated wire is generally available in white or forest green. The darker color blends well into the landscape and can make the fence nearly invisible.

Two rails will do on fences no more than 48 inches high, but you'll need a mid-rail for extra stability on higher fences. You can enhance the fence with two options: an angled cap rail that sheds water and covers the wire tips, and a pressure-treated skirt board that keeps critters from crawling under the fence.

Wood-and-Wire Basics

TOOLS
- Hammer
- Shovel
- Power drill-driver
- Electrician's pliers

MATERIALS
- ¾" U-staples
- 2" screws
- Wire fencing
- Pressure-treated 1x6 skirt board
- Posts

2 *Roll out enough wire* to reach the next post, tack the starting edge, and align the wire with the upper rail.

A basic wood-and-wire fence with rough-hewn posts can blend into a background of climbing plants and flowers.

5 *Cut the wire* with an electrician's pliers or a wire cutter. Overlap rolls by one grid on long runs.

1 **You can dig a shallow trench** to bury the bottom of the wire before, or even after, you install the rails.

3 **Once the wire is aligned,** fasten the starting edge completely with ¾-in. U-staples driven into the post.

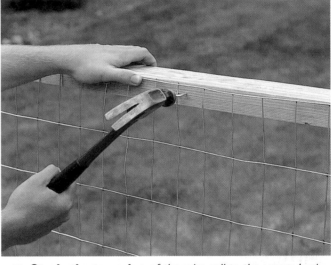

4 **Staple the top edge** of the wire roll to the upper horizontal rail. A helper can take up tension in the roll.

6 **You can cover** the ends of overlapped wire rolls by screwing a ¾-in. board to the face of the post.

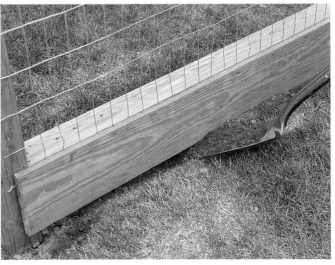

7 **Increase protection** against burrowing animals by adding a pressure-treated skirt board to the lower rail.

7

METAL FENCES

Ornamental Metal

The earliest ornamental metal fences were made of wrought iron that was heated, hammered on anvils, and twisted into curves, floral patterns, and other classic designs. These one-of-a-kind fences were largely replaced by cast iron, which allowed craftsmen to create one highly decorative mold and use it to cast many similar pieces—for example, to make many balusters for a fence or railing.

Although some craftsmen still work in wrought iron and cast iron, most ornamental metal fencing today is made of tubular steel or aluminum. You can choose from a variety of prefabricated designs and install the fence yourself, or you can have a fence custom-made and installed.

Prefabricated metal fences are generally sold through fence suppliers who can also deliver the fence to your home and install it. Designs range from ornate Victorian reproductions to sleek, modern styles. Most companies that make prefabricated fences also offer matching gates and mounting hardware.

Most prefabricated steel and aluminum fences come with a durable factory-applied finish, typically a polyester powder coating. Colors commonly available include black, white, or brown. Check the manufacturer's warranty to see how long the fence is guaranteed against rust and corrosion. If the fence you choose requires on-site painting, use a high-quality, rust-resistant paint. It often is easier to paint the components prior to installation.

With a helper or two, prefabricated metal fences are easy to install. The prefabricated panels typically come in 72- to 96-inch lengths (and various heights) and fit neatly into prepunched holes in the metal posts. You can also buy prefabricated sections and attach them to wood posts or masonry columns with mounting brackets (supplied by the manufacturer), lag screws, and masonry anchors.

Spacing between posts depends on the size of the prefabricated panels, which must fit snugly between them. For this reason, it is best to erect the fence section by section, attaching prefabricated panels after two posts are in place.

Ornamental iron fences come in many styles. You can choose a fence to accentuate your landscape or one that stands on its own.

Prefabricated Metal Installation

TOOLS

- Power drill-driver
- Rubber mallet
- Measuring tape
- Line level and 4' spirit level

MATERIALS

- Mason's twine
- Concrete
- Sheet-metal screws

1 **Post caps** and other fittings can be connected prior to installation. Use a rubber mallet to prevent marring.

2 **Secure prefabricated metal posts** in concrete, making sure that they are braced in a plumb position.

3 **Most prefab metal fences** fit together in sections. The posts are prepunched to accept rail assemblies.

4 **Secure the prefabricated rail assemblies** by fastening the tabs inserted through the slots in the posts.

Vinyl Fences

Vinyl Fencing

Vinyl fences are available in a wide variety of styles but often in only a few colors. However, they are gaining in popularity, accounting for one in five new fences, for two main reasons.

First, they are easy for most do-it-yourselfers to install because they are lightweight and sold in preformed sections that fit together without the kind of special tools and equipment you need to install some fences, such as chain-link types. Second, the vinyl is colored throughout the thickness of the material, so you don't have to paint or stain to start with and don't have to touch up little nicks or scrapes later. Because the color runs through the material, vinyl fences never need the attention that wood fences do. And vinyl won't decay, become a food source for wood-boring insects, or rust like metal fences,

Although vinyl fences generally are more expensive than the same styles in wood, manufacturers say the higher initial cost is offset by longer life and lower maintenance costs.

Usually, you buy the fence in what amounts to a kit that contains precut posts, rails, and siding. Lattice and other special features, including matching gates and mounting hardware, are also available. The components usually come in precut lengths, but you can cut them with a hacksaw or a fine-toothed handsaw.

Vinyl fences in traditional picket designs often look about the same as painted wood components.

Vinyl Fence Parts

Slotted Post

Post Cap

Upper Support Rail

Pickets

Grooved Lower Rail

Lattice

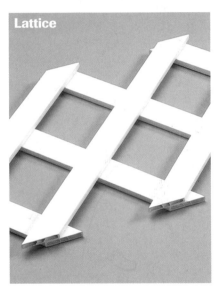

Lattice Trim Cap

Locking Rings

Splines, Screws, Caps

Vinyl Fence Styles

Vinyl can be formed into almost any style of fence that you can build out of wood, including board, rail, and picket, and combinations generally found only with wooden lattice or ornamental metal.

Vinyl fencing usually must be ordered directly from manufacturers or their distributors. The fences come in limited colors—most often white, brown, and tan—but you can dress up most installations with post caps and other decorative features modeled after Victorian, Georgian, and other styles.

You can't mix and match components from different manufacturers. But large suppliers offer options, such as a mid-rail that accepts vinyl boards or pickets below and lattice above. And some vinyl-fence designs allow you to step the installation down a slope, although you will need longer posts than you would use for a conventional project. Many assemblies can also be purposely racked to follow ground contours. Order end posts, which have holes on one side only, for all of the fence posts that will step down the hill.

Vinyl styles include offset pickets and decorative post caps.

Solid-panel vinyl fencing can step up slopes between posts to create a sheltered and private yard or garden.

Vinyl Fence Design Options

Crossbuck

Alternating-Height Picket

3-Rail

Wood-grain

Decorative Picket

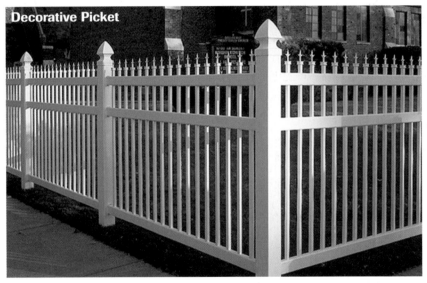

Lattice top

Open Rail

Alternating Panels

Installing Vinyl

On most vinyl installations the pieces you need to assemble are stock lengths designed to fit into slots in posts or tracks in rails without cutting. You can, of course, cut as needed to modify the stock sizes.

Basic assembly procedures vary among manufacturers. For example, some may use a locking ring to clip rails into posts, while other companies advise you simply to insert the rail and lock it in place by adding the next post in line. In any case, it's wise to look over the instructions carefully and test assemble a few of the basic components.

Most often, you fit the rails into mortises or holes cut into the hollow posts and secure the rails with screws, clips, or locking rings. The rails are also hollow and may have channels for simulated boards or mortises for pickets. Vinyl can be formed to accommodate many components, including mid-rails through which you can slide pickets and grooved rails that conceal the ends of lattice.

Installation Sequence

Using vinyl won't make digging any easier, of course. You have to start with a careful layout and use a posthole digger or power auger to make postholes. Set the posts according to the routed hole for the lower rail in each post. Because the components are already

Vinyl Fence Basics

TOOLS

- Shovel
- Hammer
- Drill-driver
- 2' spirit level
- Mason's trowel
- Measuring tape

MATERIALS

- Mason's twine
- 1x2s for stakes
- 2x4s for braces
- Screws
- Concrete mix
- Mixing trough

3 **Set the post,** and measure up from the ground to the mortise to set the clearance of the lower rail.

4 **Use two braces** set and staked at 90 deg. to each other. Clamp the upper ends to allow for adjustments.

Assembly Jig

Handling many fence parts at the same time can be difficult. Just when you have several boards or pickets coming together in a subassembly, they can fall out of position. A simple assembly jig (or a pair of them) helps. The base is a 2x4 or 2x6 a few feet long for stability. Two short pieces serve as holding blocks. Screw them to the base, allowing just enough room for the base rail between. The jig will hold the section upright as you assemble the pieces.

1 *Use strings and stakes* to lay out the fence lines. Check for square at the corners and mark the postholes.

2 *You can use a shovel* to get started, but a posthole digger is more efficient on deep holes.

5 *Check the post with a level,* and loosen the clamps to shift the post into a plumb position.

6 *Once the post is plumbed* you can add concrete (and sometimes rebar) according to manufacturer's directions.

8

VINYL FENCES

Continued on pg. 90

formed, you must add fill under posts as needed to make sure that the rails will be level. Once you firm up the post, you can add rails. (Some systems require concrete and rebar in the post hollows.) With many vinyl fences you can assemble subcomponents, such as rails and boards, and join them as a unit to the posts.

Many vinyl systems use a locking ring or similar clip system to fasten the rails into the posts. To use a locking ring, you compress it and fit it into the end of a rail. The two protruding lugs extend through holes in the rail. As you fit the rail into the post, press on the lugs, which will emerge again inside the post and keep the rail from pulling out.

Other components, including most vinyl boards,

may be joined with splines, which are rods that lock panels together. But many components simply fit together with hand pressure.

On most picket fences, for example, the bottom rail is U-shaped and the upper rail is through-mortised. Once the rails are leveled and secure, you simply slide pickets one after another through the mortises and tuck them into the groove of the bottom rail.

Some rail systems have internal stiffeners to make a strong connection with other components. To keep these from shifting, you drive a screw through the assembly. Manufacturers that use this system provide small decorative caps matched to the fencing that easily snap onto the screws and conceal the heads.

Continued from pg. 89

7 **When the concrete has set,** *insert the rails or complete subassemblies, and add the next post.*

8 **As you secure the next post,** *check the lower rail with a level. On slightly sloping ground you can rack the rails.*

11 **Fit the bottoms of the boards** *in the lower rail, and cover the top edges with a mid-rail.*

12 **On this fence design** *you may need to install a U-shaped channel on the mid-rail to hold the lattice.*

Combinations of different vinyl styles can define yards, provide privacy, and blend in with older homes.

9 **Panel sections** on many vinyl fences are joined with a spline that you insert into the edge of the panel.

10 **With the spline inserted,** you can join one plank to another. Planks are often grooved to resemble boards.

13 **You can trim vinyl lattice to size** with a sharp saw or utility knife, and slide it into the mid-rail groove.

14 **Insert the top rail** over the lattice and into the post mortise, and fit a decorative cap on the post.

Specialty
Fences

Special-Use Fences

Most house styles and sites look best with a traditional fence design, such as a horizontal-board or picket fence. But there are many other types, including basic utility fencing, barbed wire, electronic fencing for pets or livestock, fences made out of plants and other natural materials, and even fences made of recycled materials, such as one-of-a-kind fences that use old chair rungs for balusters.

■ **Utility Fencing.** Utility fencing consists of wooden slats wired together. It is sold in large rolls, in heights from 36 to 72 inches. You simply unroll the fencing and nail or wire it to wood or metal posts. While not especially attractive or durable, utility fencing can provide a temporary barrier for people and animals. Utility fencing is also called snow fencing because you can place it strategically to prevent wind-blown snow from drifting across walks or driveways.

■ **Wire Pickets.** Wire picket fencing (also sold in rolls at home centers) is used as a low temporary or decorative border around planting beds and walks. These welded-wire fences are either factory painted or vinyl coated and come in heights from 12 to 18 inches. To install, you simply unroll the wire and set it into the ground. You can also find low picket sections made of wood or PVC plastic.

■ **Rope or Chain Fences.** These easy-to-install fences make attractive, economical boundary markers along paths, walks, and driveways. These fences are popular in coastal areas because they lend a nautical feeling to the landscape. To make one, drill holes through low 4x4 or 6x6 posts and thread through a length of chain or heavy rope.

■ **Barbed Wire and Wire Mesh.** Used mainly to contain animals, both types are easy to install. With wire mesh, which is available in many gauges and sizes, you unroll and staple it to the posts. Barbed wire, which has to be handled carefully, normally comes on spools. Some pastures are bounded with mesh on posts, with a top strand of barbed wire. While barbs can be a strong deterrent to thin-skinned animals, large cows and bulls use it for scratching and can walk right through strands of barbed wire if they have the urge.

On the following pages you will also find details on hidden electric fences for pets, and the aboveground version often used around barns to contain livestock.

Posts and chains can define walkways and parking areas.

Utility fences can hold back leaves and drifting snow.

Barbed wire between posts can make an economical boundary.

Build a one-of-a-kind fence with bent strands of wood and woven wicker, complete with decorative finials on the posts.

You can use unusual recycled materials, such as old chair legs, in a decorative fence to define outdoor areas.

Pet Fences

To keep your pet at hand and safely in control, you need a fence in your yard and a leash when you're out for a walk. There have been a few improvements in both types of pet control, although some of the updates can have unexpected drawbacks.

In the leash department, for example, there's the long type that winds up on a reel and allows a dog to run far away without actually running away. Dog and master can be yards apart and seem like independent parties to innocent bystanders—until the dog sweeps past on the flank and trips them in the tether. Some dogs are very good at this game of bowling for bystanders.

What may seem like the latest development in pet control (actually in existence since the 1970s) is the electronic fence that's not really a fence. It does away with leashes (at home at least) and penned-in runs by creating electronic boundaries. Hidden electronic fence systems are commonly used around the perimeter of a yard. But you also can install them inside the house to keep pets out of particular areas.

System Components

Hidden-fence products have three main components: wires buried in shallow trenches around your property, a battery-powered collar with a receiver for your pet, and a controller that sends electromagnetic signals along the wires that are picked up by the collar.

The electronic system creates a fencelike boundary, but your pet can't see it to climb through, jump over, or tunnel under. So far, at least, there is no electronic version of a leash that extends invisible control beyond your yard.

At first blush, the fence systems come off like a force field on an old Star Trek program—a magically strong but invisible wall off which your dog will bounce. Manufacturers' literature often reinforces the image of hidden fences as a kind of space-age doghouse in which modern technology takes the place of chain link and electromagnetic waves put an end to swats with a rolled-up newspaper.

Electric-Fence Realities

Companies in the field have positive-sounding names such as Contain-a-Pet, DogWatch, PetSafe, and Invisible Fence, and their brochures focus on the benign beeping sound that warns your dog (or cat or almost any other pet) of the approaching boundary.

But the electronic doghouse isn't exactly benign and, in the end, delivers an electric shock to get the message across.

Industry literature says that proper training is the key to these systems, and generally claims a 98 percent or better success rate in keeping pets at home. But read further, and you're likely to find a more nitty-gritty section about how system controls and settings allow you to "give a stronger warning by increasing the rate of the electrical stimulation."

It's hard to find any literature that describes this fine point in plain language: that the system delivers

Invisible Pet Fence Kit Components

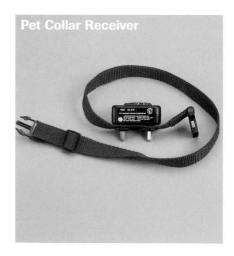

Pet Collar Receiver

Transformer and Controller

Boundary Wire

an electrical shock that hurts enough to keep your pet from bolting. But some companies are more straight-forward than others about the subject and suggest that you may want to check with a veterenarian before using an electrical restraint system.

The other side of this issue is pretty simple: that an electric jolt is well worth keeping your dog from stray-ing into the street and being hit by a car.

Basic Installation

Because the boundary wires are hidden under-ground, the systems can save you from adding a fence where you don't want one. You don't have to chop up a large yard with a fenced-in run or install a nearly solid boundary fence that sometimes can cause prob-lems with neighbors.

The systems can be tailored to fit properties rang-ing from ¼ acre to more than 20 acres, so you can cre-ate a safe area in part of the yard, simply follow your property lines, or create a combination plan that cov-ers the perimeter and creates specific internal no-pet zones as well. You can also install the electronic boundaries around trees, over steep hills, and even under water across a stream or pond.

You should start with a map of the project, such as the one shown at right, to deal with the obvious catch to the system, namely, that if you have to run wires from a transformer in your house or garage out to the perimeter of the property, how will your pet cross those lines? The solution is to twist together the two wires that carry the electricity. This defeats the

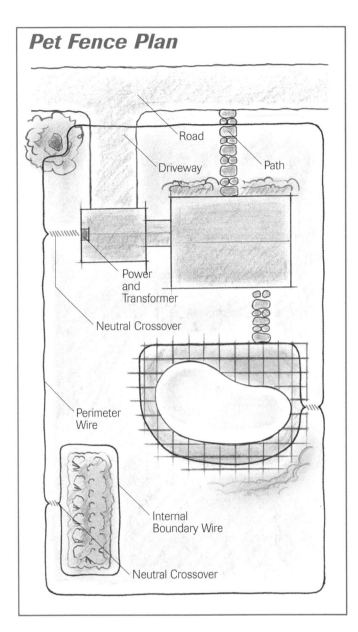

Pet Fence Plan

Road

Driveway

Path

Power and Transformer

Neutral Crossover

Perimeter Wire

Internal Boundary Wire

Neutral Crossover

System On-Off Key

Wire Marking Flags

Instructions and Training Video

charge, and creates a neutral line that pets can cross without receiving a signal.

One sensible approach is to make the two wires run along the shortest stretch from the transformer to the boundary. But you can twist wires at other points in the overall plan—for example, to bring the boundary wires back into the yard to zone off a garden or swimming pool.

Most homeowners can handle these projects on their own, although many suppliers offer professional installation. You can buy basic component kits, do the trenching work for the boundary wires, and make the straightforward electrical connections.

Generally, the wires need to be only a few inches belowground, while the controller can plug into a standard outlet in your basement or garage. Many systems come with a video that covers both installation and pet training.

Costs vary widely depending on the installation, but some basic kits start at about $200. On large properties where trenches for wires extend great distances and may have to be channeled around many obstacles, the excavation work (even for relatively shallow trenches) will be most of the job.

Where your pet is concerned, installation consists of buckling on a battery-powered collar. Most weigh between 1 and 2 ounces, and are suitable for Great Danes, Chihuahuas, and cats of all sizes.

Unexpected Effects

Manufacturers understandably do not make a point of listing the drawbacks of their products. But there are a few, aside from the somewhat controversial point of delivering electric shocks to your pet. For example, some generally satisfied hidden-fence homeowners say that the shock treatment can have a negative effect on the personality of the pet. Another problem seems to be that while trainable and naturally docile or timid dogs always stop short of the electronic boundary, some more spirited animals do not.

Take the case reported by a homeowner of a dog that regularly chases rabbits out of instinct or entertainment. The owner says it's become an obsession even though he never catches them no matter how hard he tries. The urge is so strong that the dog will bolt at full speed right through the electronic barrier in pursuit. The problem is that after he calms down he won't cross the barrier to come home.

Pet Fence Basics

TOOLS
- Circular saw
- Masonry cutting blade
- Shovel
- Power drill-driver
- Wire strippers or lineman's pliers
- Safety glasses
- Dust mask

MATERIALS
- Pet fence kit

3 **Spool out boundary wire,** and run it in the perimeter trenches to make a continuous loop of the property.

6 **Bring the twisted crossover lead** from the transformer, and connect and tape it to the boundary line.

1 **Dig a shallow trench** for boundary and crossover wires. Generally, you can simply replace the same sod.

2 **Cross driveways and walks** by cutting a narrow channel with a circular saw and masonry-cutting blade.

4 **To close the loop,** strip insulation off the ends of the boundary line, join them, and tape the connection.

5 **Form twisted crossover lines** by spinning strands with a drill. Protect the wire in the chuck with tape.

7 **Strip the crossover lead,** install the transformer, and connect the wires per the manufacturer's instructions.

8 **Check the system** to be sure the circuit is working. Bury the wires, and resod the trenches.

9

SPECIALTY FENCES

Livestock Fences

Different animals require different types of fences. For example, horse farms usually install expensive post-and-board fences, while cattle or dairy farms usually go with a few strands of barbed or high-tensile wire. Poultry and small animals are kept in place with woven wire or chicken wire, and goats, noted for their ability to outsmart a fence, may required an eight-strand electrified fence with a 12-volt charger.

Aside from welded wire and barbed wire (which may be restricted from use in residential areas), livestock fencing often consists of economical high-tensile wire strung along a line of rustic posts. It can be electrified, but this job generally requires professional expertise to create a safe, code-approved system matched to the livestock you need to contain.

If an electrified fence is necessary, you can use one that is direct wired or a system suited to remote locations that is battery powered or even solar powered. Bear in mind that, unlike other fences, electrified fences must be kept free of weeds, branches, or anything else that might cause a short-circuit.

High-Tensile Wire

This steel wire has high strength and resiliency, but often is attached to springs at the ends of long runs to allow tightening and keep it from breaking if a branch falls on the fence. The wire is available in various gauges, in a galvanized or aluminum-clad finish (aluminum being longer lasting) to prevent corrosion, and rated by breaking strength, generally between 120,000 and 200,000 pounds per square inch.

Each run has a corner lag, which attaches the wire to the post, and mounts at intermediate posts. Most installations also have springs. For an electrified fence, the corner lag and intermediate mounts must be insulated so that the posts don't ground the system.

The basic procedure is to drill pilot holes in the end posts and turn in the lags. Then cut a piece of wire about 18 inches long, loop it around the lag, and twist the end around the wire at least 8 to 10 times. Attach the end of this wire to one of the loops on the end of a spring, and twist it on there as well. Attach the lead of the long run to the other end of the spring. Then attach the fence strainer to the end of this wire, apply tension, fasten the wire to the spring mount, and lag this end of the run.

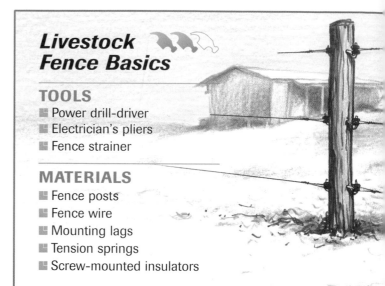

Livestock Fence Basics

TOOLS
- Power drill-driver
- Electrician's pliers
- Fence strainer

MATERIALS
- Fence posts
- Fence wire
- Mounting lags
- Tension springs
- Screw-mounted insulators

2 **Twist the mounting lag by hand** into the pilot hole. This lag has an insulator suitable for electrification.

5 **On long runs,** install a tension spring between the lag-end wires and the main run, twisting over all connections.

1 ***Drill a pilot hole*** *for each mounting lag in the side of the post. Use a string and line level over long runs.*

3 ***Loop an 18-in. length of high-tensile wire*** *around the lag (or electrical insulator) for each strand in the run.*

4 ***Secure the wire to the lag*** *by making 8 to 10 twists. You can use an electrician's pliers to cut off any excess.*

6 ***On intermediate posts*** *you can fit the wire between the guides of a small screw-mounted insulator.*

7 ***Use a ratchet-style fence strainer*** *to take up tension and secure the end-run loop to the second spring.*

9

SPECIALTY FENCES

Gates

Gate Design

According to an old adage, gates can tell you a lot about the people who live behind them. Gates can be simple or ornate, formal or rustic, traditional or contemporary, inviting or forbidding. The gate should complement the fence design but can break away from the uniform row of pickets or boards, which creates almost limitless possibilities.

To call attention to an opening, choose a design that contrasts with the surrounding fence. A low ornamental metal gate, for example, can soften the imposing mass of a solid masonry wall. Similarly, you can call attention to the gate by changing the size, spacing, or direction of the siding materials used on the fence. If you want privacy, gates leading to side yards or backyards, for example, can be constructed from the same materials as the fence to give the impression of an unbroken barrier.

■ **Gate Materials.** Most gates are made of wood or ornamental metal. You can choose from a variety of prefabricated designs or create your own. No matter what design you choose, the gate must be sturdy enough to swing freely without sagging or binding. The most successful wooden gates use lightweight, kiln-dried wood and heavy-duty hinges, and have sufficient bracing to prevent sagging.

■ **Gate Size and Weight.** Spacing between gate posts should be 36 to 48 inches. Generally, posts for gates leading to a house front door should be 48 inches apart, which allows room for two people to pass through at once. Posts for gates leading to backyards or side yards should be spaced no less than 36 inches apart so that lawn mowers and other wheeled garden equipment fit through the opening.

Even for low gates, you need to set the posts a minimum of 24 inches in the ground, or below the frost line in cold climates. Plumb both posts.

If you're installing a prefabricated gate, space the posts to provide clearance on the latch side and hinge side. In most cases, ½ inch of clearance on the hinge side and ½ to ¾ inch on the latch side will do. But you should use the clearances specified by the gate manufacturer. The clearances required for chain-link and

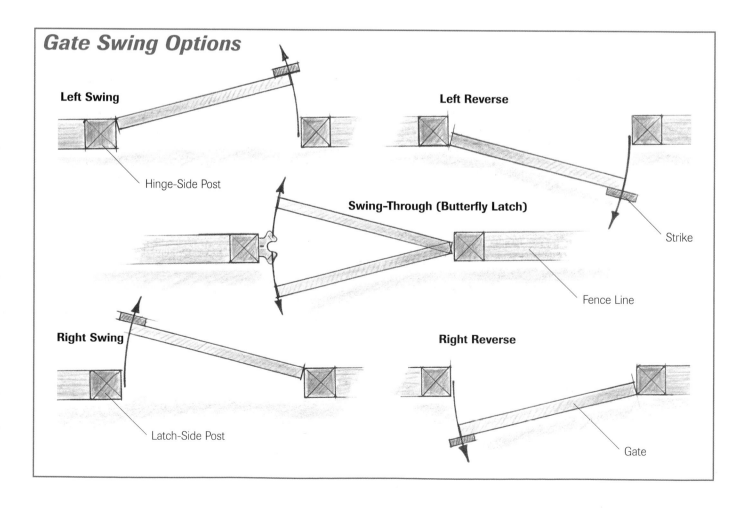

Gate Swing Options

Left Swing

Hinge-Side Post

Left Reverse

Strike

Swing-Through (Butterfly Latch)

Fence Line

Right Swing

Latch-Side Post

Right Reverse

Gate

ornamental metal gates are usually determined by the type of hardware used to attach them.

Usually, gates are the same height as the fence or wall, but not necessarily. The gate's height depends on its function and on the fence design. If a fence or wall provides security and privacy, make the gate the same height and as difficult to climb as the adjacent wall.

Keep the weight of the gate in mind when choosing materials. The gate should be sturdy enough to stand up to continuous use but not so heavy that it's hard to open and close. Large, solid-board gates tend to be heavy and may require three or even four hinges to support them. If the gate swings over a smooth masonry walk, you can install a wheel on the bottom of a heavy gate to relieve strain on the hinges and to keep the gate from sagging.

Gate Location. Usually, gates are located where a fence or wall will cross an existing or proposed walkway or entry. In a new landscape, these elements are planned simultaneously as part of the overall scheme.

If you are installing a front boundary fence directly next to a sidewalk (especially a busy one), it is good practice to jog the fence back 36 to 48 inches from the sidewalk and install the gate there. Setting the gate back from the sidewalk provides an area where you can conveniently open and close the gate away from any traffic on the sidewalk.

Gate Swing. Entry gates traditionally open in toward the house. There is no set rule for gates, but your front door swings inward, which is generally the best design that invites entry instead of impeding it. And, somehow, pulling a gate toward you makes more sense as you're leaving.

The direction of swing also can depend on features near the gate. For example, if the gate crosses a sloping walk, it may have to swing downhill to provide clearance at the bottom of the gate. If a gate is located at the corner of a fence or at a wall, it is usually best to have the gate swing toward the structure. You can attach a hook to the structure and a screw eye to the gate to keep the gate open when necessary.

Some gates can be installed to swing through the opening, such as a chain-link gate that can be held by a two-way butterfly latch.

Gate-Closing Hardware

Gates may swing freely on their hinges, and, of course, it's easy enough to push a gate open as you walk through the opening. But why wait to turn around and fumble with pulling it closed when you can install hardware to close the gate automatically? There are several types of spring-loaded hinges, including spring additions to standard hinges (left)

and the most common type, simply a spring with screw-mounted ends (right). As you open the gate, there is slight resistance as the energy is stored in the spring. After you walk through, the energy is released and the gate closes. Some people install spring-loaded hinges and adjust the tension so that the gate stays closed against a strike without a latch.

Gate Hardware

Hinges and latches range from utilitarian to ornamental. Choose a style that is appropriate for the fence design, and consider whether you will mount hardware on the face or edge of the gate.

■ **Hinges.** There are four basic hinge types: butt hinges, T-hinges, strap hinges, and pin-and-strap hinges. Make sure they are designed for exterior use and are heavy enough to support the weight of the gate. A good rule is to choose the heaviest hinges you can install that are still in visual scale with the gate.

■ **Gate Latches.** You have many choices when it comes to gate latches. Most will work no matter how you build the gate to swing. Some latches are designed to be fitted with a padlock, or you can install a separate lock and hasp. On seldom-used gates, a hasp alone may suffice. Formal door-style gates, such as those leading to a courtyard or front-entry enclosure, can be fitted with conventional door locksets.

■ **Sag Rods.** On wide or heavy gates, it's wise to use sag rods or cables with adjustable turnbuckles to keep gates from sagging or binding. Install them diagonally with the high end of the rod or cable at the top post hinge and the bottom of the rod fastened to the bottom corner of the gate.

■ **Gate Springs.** Make your gate close automatically with the help of a gate spring. One bracket mounts to the gate, the other to the fence.

A wrought-iron thumb latch is traditional with picket designs.

Sag Rods for Gates

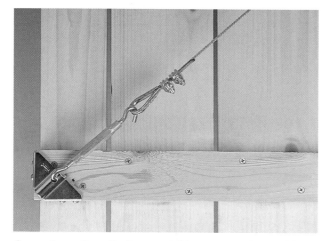

Sag rods run from the lower outside corner to the top hinge.

Turnbuckles allow you to increase tension over time.

Gate-Hinge Options

Butt Hinge

T-Hinge

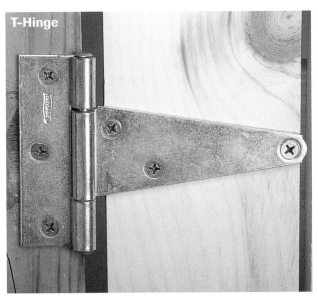

Strap Hinge

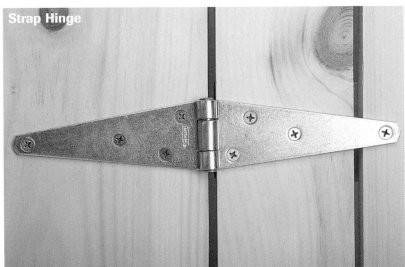

Mortised Butt Hinge

Ornamental T-Hinge

Ornamental Pin-Mount Hinge

10 GATES

Gate Latches

There are many types of hardware that will secure a gate. They range from a basic hook-and-eye, which can be somewhat inconvenient on a gate that's used frequently, to hasps that you can secure with a padlock. There are also several types of sliding bolts and traditional wrought-iron latches. You can install some types in combination with a spring-loaded hinge to close and latch automatically.

There are other alternatives, of course. One is to limit the gate swing with a strike, install a spring-loaded hinge, and use any type of decorative nob (on both sides) to easily grasp the gate.

Another approach is to build your own custom latch, such as the one shown below. You can make one out of 1x4 pine. Round over or simply sand the edges, and apply several coats of sealer or stain to protect it from the weather.

The idea is to build three keepers through which a horizontal latch bar can slide. Two of the keepers are fastened to the gate, and one to the adjacent post. With a dowel or some other type of handle between the two gate-mounted keepers, you can slide the latch back and forth across the opening to the post keeper. As the handle protrudes, the latch won't slide free.

Making a Custom Sliding Latch

Find the center of the sliding latch board, and scribe an arc that rounds the end to prevent it from catching.

Cut the arc on the end of the latch board. This helps it slide freely through the post-mounted keeper.

Make keeper assemblies by predrilling and screwing a cover piece on blocks the same thickness as the latch.

Level the three keepers (two on the gate and one on the post), slide in the latch board, and add a dowel handle.

Gate Latch Options

Hook-and-Eye

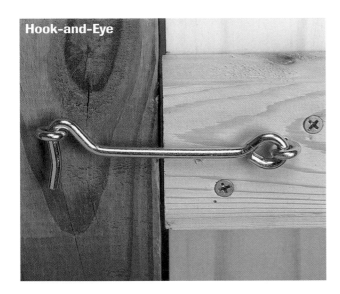

Thumb Latch

Barrel Bolt

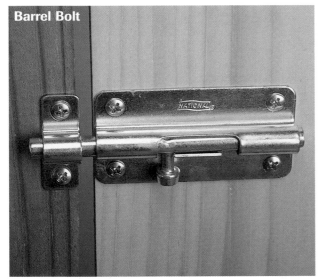

Locking Hasp

Decorative Thumb Latch

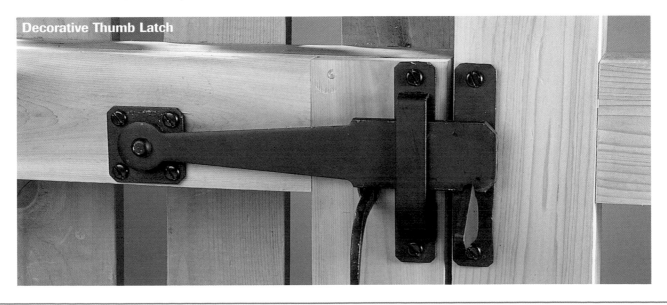

Basic Gate Frames

Most wooden gates are built from a braced frame of 2x4s to which you attach the siding of your choice. But before you start building, it is a good idea to spend some time checking the posts that will support the gate.

With a level, double-check to make sure the fence posts on either side of your gate opening are plumb. Then measure the distance between posts at both the top and the bottom, and make sure the distance is the same. If a post is misaligned, either reposition it with a sag rod or take it out and reset it. You should leave about 1 inch extra between the gate posts to allow clearance for the gate hinges and latch.

You can build a basic gate frame with butt joints at the corners, more-sturdy half-laps, or more elegant miters. Because a gate takes a lot of stress, it's wise to use screws instead of nails, predrilling to avoid splits. You can also add strength by reinforcing the corners with hardware and by adding at least one cross brace to prevent racking and to build in resistance to sagging.

If you are applying pickets or other boards to the face of the gate frame, you can screw standard angle iron braces across the joints. (Always check the frame with a square first.) You can also install L-shape braces on the interior of the frame. One diagonal brace will help. But two, joined with half-laps to form an X-shape, provide the most strength.

Framing a Gate

TOOLS
- Power drill-driver
- Screwdriver bit
- Pencil
- Circular saw
- Safety glasses
- Measuring tape
- Chisel
- Framing square

MATERIALS
- Metal L-brackets
- Pickets
- 2x4s
- Galvanized screws

1 **Square up the frame,** predrill at the ends of the boards at each corner to avoid splits, and drive two screws.

4 **The brace should tuck snugly** between corners. You can fasten it with angled metal braces bent to fit.

5 **Make complementary half-laps** in a pair of diagonal braces to keep both boards flush with the gate frame.

Frame Corner Options

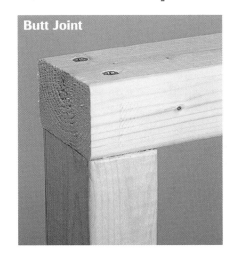

Butt Joint

Half-Lap Joint

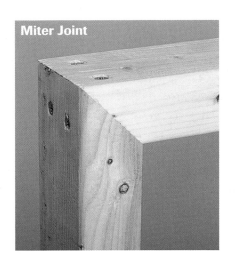

Miter Joint

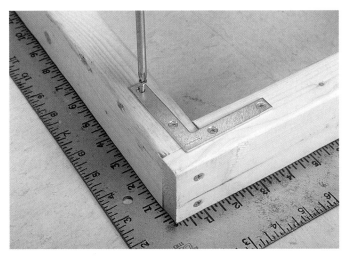

2 *Double-check the corner* with a framing square before screwing down an L-shaped brace across the joint.

3 *To install a diagonal brace,* set a straight 2x4 corner to corner and mark the V-shaped end.

6 *Secure the half-lap with a screw.* Also strengthen joints by using exterior-grade construction adhesive.

7 *Test-fit* the pickets or other boards to create an evenly spaced exterior to the gate frame; then fasten them.

Solid Gates

Widely spaced pickets make a gate lightweight. But with solidly mounted hinges you can safely add more lumber, such as tongue-and-groove pine or simple boards butted against each other on the gate frame. Of course, the weight is distributed differently on a gate than it is on the rest of the fence because gates don't have supporting posts on both sides. The weight is transferred through the gate frame onto a single, hinge-side post, so you need to take the post's design into account when you plan the gate.

You may want to switch from the 4x4s used along the fence line, for example, and install 6x6 posts for the gate. This kind of step up in scale generally looks appropriate on most fences and highlights the passageway through the fence.

You may be able to space boards the way they are spaced on the fence. More often, you have to adjust them to fit the opening. Do this by setting full boards in the center of the gate and splitting the difference with two boards ripped to equal widths for the ends.

Custom gate designs can create an unusual entry.

Joining Gate Boards with a

Lay out boards with spacers, and square up the gate. Cut equal-sized end boards to make the layout symmetrical.

Diagonal Board Gate

TOOLS
- Combination square
- Framing square
- Power drill-driver
- Pencil
- Screwdriver bit
- Predrill and countersink bits

MATERIALS
- Tongue-and-groove boards
- 1x6 pine
- 1" galvanized screws

3 **Mark the angle** on each diagonal board, and cut to fit. You can also screw all boards down and cut them at once.

Z-Brace

Use a 2x3 or 2x4 top and bottom for back bracing. Predrill, countersink, and drive two screws for each board.

Cut the angles on a diagonal brace to complete the Z-shape. Run the brace up from the lower-hinge side.

1 **Lay out and square up the gate frame,** *allowing about 1 in. of clearance for the hinges and latch.*

2 **Secure the corners** *with triangular gussets. You can also use ornamental hardware or concealed biscuits.*

4 **Face the gate** *with a band of boards. Secure the boards with a series of screws in a staggered pattern.*

5 **Complete the gate** *by screwing on a pine strip that covers the end grain of the diagonal boards.*

Lattice-Panel Gates

You can use lattice to create a light, airy gate. But a large panel of stock material is a bit flimsy for a gate that will get a lot of use, and you will probably need one or more intermediate braces for support. A couple of beefy 2x4 braces will show through and detract from the airy appearance, however.

There are two good options that beat this problem. One is to fabricate your own lattice out of one-by lumber that has enough strength to span a gate without extra braces.

Another approach is to make most of the gate from solid boards, spaced or set against each other, and then add a narrow panel of stock lattice across the top, where it is held in place with nailers around the inside of the frame.

Because it combines two styles, this gate will take longer to build than other gates. However, no special skills or tools are required. The gate is also relatively heavy, so purchase strong hinges. If you want to make it lighter, use 2x3s for the frame instead of 2x4s, or purchase lightweight lumber, such as kiln-dried redwood or cedar.

Also buy or rip enough nailers to create two sets of perimeter bands inside the frame. They sandwich the lattice and boards. Nail them so that both the boards and the lattice will be centered in the gate frame.

Hinging to Masonry

Wood-to-wood connections are easy to make. Fastening a gate post to masonry is more difficult. You need to drill through the post, set it in position, and mark the hole locations. Then you drill a hole in the masonry and insert an anchor that will capture the threads of screws or bolts that hold the post. You can dig out a hole by hand, but it's easier with a drill and masonry bit, or a rotary hammer drill. You can also use (or rent) a gun that fires hardened nails into masonry.

Hammer and Star Drill

Drill and Masonry Bit

Rotary Hammer Drill

Powder-Actuated Nailer

Heavy-Duty Gate Mounts

Perhaps the stongest and most durable gate mount is a pin-mount hinge, also called a hook-and-strap hinge. The two-part system relies on a secure and solid gate post large enough to accept the L-shape pin. Some pin hardware can be bolted through the thickness of the post, while most simply screw in. The adjoining gate hinge, which can be a long, decorative leaf (right) or a short metal arm (far right), has an eye that transfers weight onto the pin.

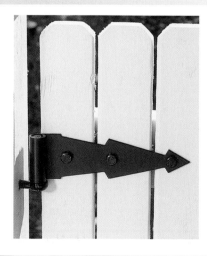

Lattice Gate

TOOLS

- Power drill-driver
- Hammer
- Circular saw
- Framing square
- Safety glasses
- Measuring tape

MATERIALS

- Lattice panel
- Tongue-and-groove boards
- 2x4s
- One-by rippings
- Galvanized finishing nails
- 16d nails

1 **Frame up the gate** out of 2x4s, including an extra cross piece about a foot down from the top rail.

2 **Use wood blocks** to support nailing strips at their proper recessed position around the inside of the frame.

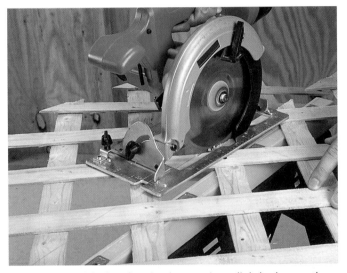

3 **Set the blade** of a circular saw just slightly deeper than the thickness of the lattice to trim the panel to size.

4 **Tack the lattice** in place in the upper frame, and cut boards to fit against the nailers in the lower section.

5 **Finish off the installation** by adding a second layer of nailing strips to cover the ends of the lattice and boards.

10 GATES

Hanging a Gate

The key part of this finishing step in a fence project is to position the gate in the opening. You need to check that there will be enough room for hardware, and line up elements of the gate and fence, such as horizontal rails and frames, as needed.

The easiest approach is to set the gate up on a few boards, and use a combination of spacers and shingle shims to adjust it in the opening between posts. Use clamps or other braces as needed so that the gate won't move as you drill and attach hardware. Except on bank vault doors, all hinges settle a bit after installation. So add an extra shim under the latch side.

Hanging a Gate

TOOLS
- Framing square
- Pencil
- Wrench
- Slip-joint pliers
- Power drill-driver
- Combination square
- Screwdriver bit

MATERIALS
- Gate
- Hinges
- Latch
- Lag screws
- Galvanized screws
- Scrap wood
- Shingle shims

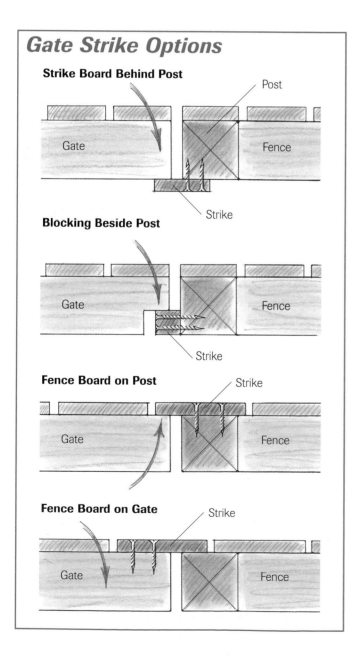

Gate Strike Options

Strike Board Behind Post

Post

Gate | Fence

Strike

Blocking Beside Post

Gate | Fence

Strike

Fence Board on Post

Strike

Gate | Fence

Fence Board on Gate

Strike

Gate | Fence

3 **The leaf side** of this heavy-duty pin-mount hinge attaches to the gate frame with three bolts.

6 **Screw the pin mount** into the support post. This gate will be mounted just inside the fence line.

1 ***Check the frame for square*** *to be sure it fits evenly in the opening. You can rack and rebrace the gate as needed.*

2 ***Prop up the gate in position,*** *and use a combination square to mark the locations of the hinges.*

4 ***Add spacers top and bottom,*** *and clamp or brace the gate in position before setting the pin-mount hinge.*

5 ***Build in a slight allowance for sagging*** *by inserting a shingle shim under the lower latch-side corner.*

7 ***Once the gate is adjusted and swinging freely,*** *you can mount a protruding strike board with screws.*

8 ***Finish the job by*** *attaching any antisag hardware and screwing on the latch and keeper.*

Finishing

Finishing Options

A finish does more than dress up your project. It provides a barrier against the weather, sheds water, discourages decay, and minimizes any checking and warping. There is a great variety of finishes to choose from, but all fall into one of four basic types.

■ **Water Sealer.** Most sealers contain a wax dissolved in mineral spirits. The wax lodges in the pores of the wood, sealing it against water. The finish is clear but will slightly darken the wood.

Water sealers are applied to all aboveground parts and reapplied annually to maintain a natural wood color. There are no sealers that will preserve the tone of new wood. Redwood, cedar, and other woods will weather even under coatings that contain a UV inhibiter to reduce fading from sunlight.

■ **Stain.** Semitransparent stains have pigment mixed with a preservative. Opaque stains offer more protection than semitransparent ones because they have more pigment in a mix that resembles paint. While neither type of stain is as durable as paint, stains do not crack or peel as paint does. Better yet, when it comes time to apply fresh stain in a few years, you won't have to scrape and brush off the old finish. Check the label to make sure that the stain is for exterior use and provides protection against mildew and UV rays.

■ **Varnish.** Varnish is a combination of an oil and a resin. It is durable, though prone to cracking and flaking. Polyurethane is the toughest of the varnish types but not the best for exterior use. Direct sunlight can cause polyurethane to peel, and repairs are almost impossible. These finishes are best used indoors on floors and furniture. Outside, use a spar or marine-grade varnish that has a higher oil content.

■ **Paint.** Paint is an excellent wood preservative because it forms a surface film that seals the wood against moisture. The drawback is that you have to scrape and repaint periodically. You can use water-based acrylic latex or oil-based alkyd. Latex cleans up with soap and water. Alkyd requires paint thinner. Both types come in flat, semigloss (satin), and gloss. Better exterior paints include mildewcides that inhibit the growth of mold and decay-causing organisms.

Finishing Pressure-Treated Wood

Pressure-treating wood protects it from insects and rot but does not prevent cupping or warping. So you should protect the wood with a finish. Unfortunately, pressure-treated wood presents some finishing problems. The treatment puts moisture back into the wood, sometimes leaving a waterlogged surface that just won't hold a finish. Before you apply a finish to pressure-treated wood, sprinkle a few drops of water on it. If the wood absorbs the water, it is ready to finish. If not, you should wait until air circulation dries out some of the moisture.

Semitransparent oil-based stains generally work best over pressure-treated wood. Another option is to coat the wood annually with a water sealer. Most manufacturers advise against painting pressure-treated wood with latex paint.

Wood Weathering Comparisons

Spruce New

Spruce Old

Cedar New

Cedar Old

A clear sealer or neutral penetrating stain finish preserves and protects the natural look of wood.

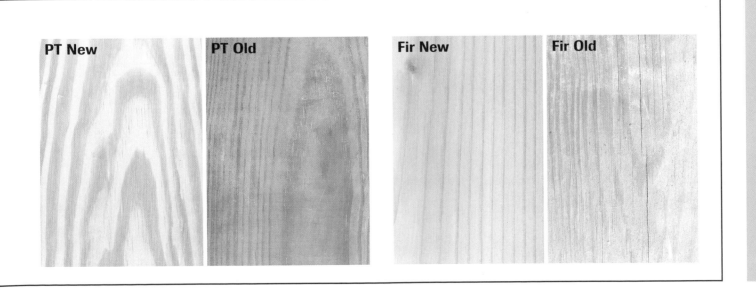

PT New

PT Old

Fir New

Fir Old

Applying Finishes

You can apply any type of finish or preservative with a brush, roller, or spray gun. While brushing is the most time consuming, it is often the best method for painting or staining fences with spaced boards or pickets. Rollers work well for fences with solid-board or plywood siding, but you'll still need a brush to reach areas that the roller misses.

Spray guns can work well for designs that would be time consuming to paint with a brush and roller, such as those with latticework or basket weave. But a spray gun will not save much time when painting an open design, such as a post-and-rail fence, and you'll end up wasting more paint than you would with a brush and roller. You will also need to spread drop cloths or drape plastic sheeting to prevent overspray from damaging nearby plants.

Redwood and cedar are expensive, elegant woods, so they're often stained or left to weather naturally. But some people paint these woods, especially if they're using cheaper or rougher grades. Both species bleed, which means that brownish-red tannins in the wood will seep through light-colored paints and discolor the finish. To prevent bleeding on freshly milled redwood, cedar, or even pine, apply one or two coats of stain-blocking primer to all knots and other areas that might bleed. Follow with a coat of alkyd primer to thoroughly seal the wood. If bleeding is not a concern, simply apply an alkyd or latex primer to all sides of any bare wood.

Semitransparent stain can provide an evenly weathered look.

Stained and Painted Finishes

Clear Sealer

Clear sealer protects wood and lets the grain show through.

Semitransparent Stain

Semitransparent stain adds a hue over the wood grain.

Decorative Hardware Details

Copper Cladding

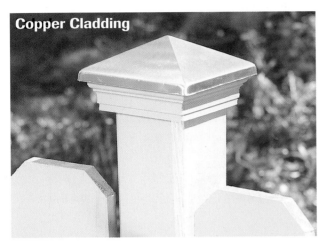

Copper caps call attention to gate posts and shed water.

Combination Hardware

Latches with oversize handles allow easy access.

Ornamental Metalwork

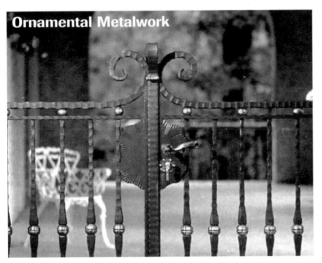

Contrasting metals create ornamental details.

Ornamental Hinges

Custom wrought-iron T-hinges can support wide gates.

Full-Bodied Stain

Full-bodied stain is opaque and covers the wood grain.

Paint (two coats)

Two coats of paint are opaque but lie on the surface.

Priming before Painting

The trend with modern exterior-grade paints is a promise of long-lasting one-coat coverage over almost any type of material in any condition, whether it's raw fencing or kiln-dried boards. To be competitive, paint manufacturers outpace each other with claims about needing only the most minimal preparation work over any surface.

But no matter what type of paint you apply, two thin coats are almost always better than one thick coat. After spot-priming blemishes with a stain killer, it may be tempting to load up a brush or roller and try to do the job in one pass. While a brush or roller loaded with penetrating stain helps more material seep into the wood grain, a single thick coat of paint is likely to drip, sag, or blister under the hot sun before it dries. And no paint is immune to dull-spotting and eventual peeling where patches of rough surface grain pull excess moisture from the fresh paint as it sets and dries.

The upshot is that it's best to prime the entire fence. That provides the most uniform surface for the top coat, particularly on rougher boards. There are special priming paints, but in most cases a layer of your top-coat paint thinned by about a third will do just as well.

If you're spraying, you would have to double back on wet areas to apply a thick coat of paint. And that can increase the chance of creating drips and sags, which is one of the drawbacks of spraying in general. If you can contain the spray, this light, once-over application can produce a reasonable prime coat.

Top-Coating Tips

For best results, always keep a wet edge so that the start of one section won't dry before you get back to continue, resulting in lap marks. This isn't a problem on fences with spaced pickets or boards, but lapping can show up on solid fences. It helps to work on manageable areas at one time to reduce the amount of wet edge and the chance of creating lap marks.

Also, always work from high to low, cutting-in seams between pickets and rails, for instance, then brushing out the surfaces so that you can pick up drips on your way down. If you work on a large area and drips have hardened, scrape them off instead of trying to blend them with fresh paint. On large projects where you start early and finish late, follow the sun around the yard so that it will have warmed up and dried the fence boards of any moisture by the time you reach them.

If you're working with water-based latex paint, remember to use a brush with nylon bristles. If you're working with oil-based alkyd paint, use a brush with natural bristles. A good tool for all-around work is a 3-inch-wide long-handled brush. It offers good control, particularly when you apply a little pressure and flex the bristles to fit into a tight spot.

You may find that it saves time and effort to use a roller for basic application and a brush for working paint into seams between boards. On pickets and spaced boards, you can use a small trim-type roller (only a few inches wide) to coat the faces and edges of boards or pickets. Follow up with a brush to work the paint into joints and brush out the surfaces.

Smart Tip PAINTING VS. SPRAYING

*P*ainting pickets with a brush can take a lot of time because you generally need two coats, and there are all those edges to cover. Spraying spreads paint faster than a brush, but overspray can be a problem. You'll need to protect nearby vegetation with plastic sheeting. The best bet may be a combination: spray on a prime coat, and use a brush to work into the nooks and crannies and brush out the top coat.

11

A painted fence can complement the colors of a house and define the approach to the front door.

Surface Preparation

I f you use boards or pickets with knots and other imperfections and don't want them to show through, apply a stain killer. Sold under various trade names, most stain killers consist of pigmented white shellac. It looks like full-strength white paint but has the ability to hide blemishes and seal knots to reduce bleeding. Spot-prime imperfections with stain killer to start. Then apply a prime coat. The top coat should completely cover the primed patches.

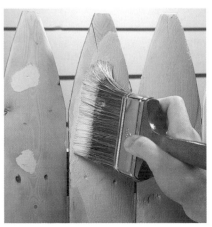

Fence Repairs

Straightening Posts

Minor out-of-plumb conditions are normal. If a small lean is bothersome, you can often fix it by pulling the post upright by hand and driving a pressure-treated stake next to it. If the post is leaning a lot, reset it.

Start by digging out enough dirt to allow the post to move. If the post is set in concrete and the foundation is tilted, you may have to break up the concrete.

In some cases it also helps to disconnect the rails and siding from a leaning post so that you don't have to pull a large section of fence along with the post. But if you use a come-along, you can pull almost any leaning post and the fence to which it's attached. Loop one end of the come-along cable around the post, or attach it to a temporary screw eye. Fasten the other cable to a nearby tree or temporary brace, such as a length of pipe driven at an angle into the ground. Crank the come-along, and the post will move.

Brace the post securely to hold the position and take some of the tension off of the come-along. Then you can backfill with tamped gravel or concrete. If you use concrete, allow it to harden for one or two days before removing the braces.

In addition to (or more typically, instead of) using concrete, you can install a diagonal brace to straighten up a post that is leaning in line with a fence. You can also install a sag rod with an adjustable turnbuckle.

Straightening a Fence Post

TOOLS
- Sledgehammer
- Shovel
- Drill-driver
- Come-along

MATERIALS
- Steel pole or stake
- Screw eye
- Brace

1 *To straighten a leaning fence,* start by widening the hole so you can move the post into an upright position.

4 *Attach one end of a come-along cable* to the fence post and the other end to the angled rod.

5 *Crank the come-along handle* to take up tension in the cable and pull the fence.

Smart Tip   PLUMBING POSTS

Plumbing posts can be challenging in situations where you need to manage a level, a brace, and a clamp at the same time. You can hold a 4-foot spirit level (near right) with one hand and clamp the brace with the other. Another option is to use a handy tool called a post level (far right). It attaches to the post and has bubble vials to plumb the post front-to-back and side-to-side as you make adjustments and add braces.

2 **Drive a steel pole** (a long 2x4 stake may do) at an angle on the side toward which you want to pull the fence.

3 **Mount a screw eye** on the main post (or loop it with cushioned cable) so that you can attach a come-along.

6 **Check the post for plumb,** and attach an angled brace on the other side to stabilize the fence.

7 **Backfill the post with concrete,** and leave one or more angled braces in place until it hardens.

Repairing Posts

Most fence repairs involve repairing or replacing one or more damaged posts. There are many types of wood problems that can weaken a post. Wood can be chewed away by insects or infected with a disease such as dry rot. But the most common problem is rot near the base of a post where water collects.

If your posts are set in gravel, dig around each one to a depth of about 4 inches. Check for decay by probing with a screwdriver, knife, or another sharp object. While you're at it, also check joints where rails meet posts and where boards attach to rails. Check exposed ends, such as tops of posts and picket boards.

If the tool sinks easily into the wood, you will have to repair or replace the post. If decay is less than about ½ inch deep into the surface, use a paint scraper or wide wood chisel to scrape out the decayed area down to sound wood, and treat the exposed wood with several coats of a good wood preservative, penetrating stain, or two coats of paint.

Rescuing Damaged Posts

If the post is rotted at or below ground level but the aboveground portion is still good, you can probably install a brace instead of replacing the post. Start by digging around the existing post down to the bottom. If the post has a concrete collar, break up the concrete using a pick or heavy pry bar, and remove the pieces.

Before you do any cutting, add at least one brace to hold the top of the post in position. Then you can cut off the damaged post about 1 to 2 inches aboveground and remove the rotted portion. You should be able to cut most of the way through with a circular saw, even without detaching the rails and siding. But you'll need to finish the cut with a handsaw or a hammer and chisel.

Make a permanent brace out of a pressure-treated post by cutting it just long enough to reach from the base of the hole to about 6 inches onto the old post. Clamp the stub piece in place, plumb the assembly, drill through both posts at the overlap, and secure the sections with at least three galvanized bolts. Cut the top end of the stub at an angle to aid water runoff.

If your fence design won't accommodate this type of brace or if you simply don't like the look of it, you can also attach pressure-treated 2x4 braces on each side of the post.

Smart Tip CHECKING FOR ROT

It doesn't take an expert to recognize that a dark brown patch of spongy looking wood near the bottom of a fence post is probably rot. But a lot of wood decay can be on the surface, leaving most of the wood intact and capable of supporting the fence. You can test the depth of rot by digging a knife into the wood. If the spongy material is only ½ inch or so deep on a 6-inch-diameter post, for example, scrape it away and apply several coats of preservative. If the knife sinks in deeply, it's probably time to replace the post.

Diagnosing Wood Problems

Carpenter ants burrow.

Powder post beetles tunnel.

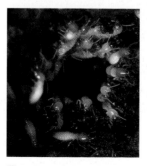
Termites also tunnel.

Carpenter bees bore holes.

Reinforcing a Post

TOOLS
- Cold chisel
- Hammer
- Saw
- Clamps
- Shovel
- Knife or screwdriver
- Drill-driver

MATERIALS
- Carriage bolts
- 4x4 post
- Concrete mix
- Nails

1 **Check for rot** *by digging into the dirt, gravel, or concrete collar to probe the wood with a knife or screwdriver.*

2 **Temporarily brace the top of the post,** *and break up the old concrete necklace or dig out the gravel backfill.*

3 **Cut off the lower, rotten section,** *and install a new stub post bottom next to the old post.*

4 **Predrill and install** *galvanized carriage bolts to lock the posts together. Angle the new post top to shed water.*

5 **Backfill the new excavation** *with concrete or tamped gravel. Leave on the brace until the concrete sets.*

12

FENCE REPAIRS

Reinforce a Loose Gate

Loose hinges are one of the most common causes of gate failure, especially if the gate is heavy and is used a lot. If the hinges have served the gate for a long time and are still in good shape, the screws may have just worked themselves loose over the years. However, premature hinge failure may be due to hinges that are too small or screws that are too short.

But gates can sag or bind for a variety of reasons: leaning posts; a racked or out-of-square gate frame; loose or bent hinges; or loose screws. There are several ways to fix these problems.

■ If the screws are loose, tighten them. If the screw holes are worn to the point that the screws no longer have a good bite, replace the screws with longer ones. If longer screws aren't feasible, epoxy small dowels into the old screw holes. When the epoxy dries, reattach the hinges. If necessary, you can remove the hinges and relocate them slightly above or below their original position on the gate and post so that you'll be fastening to new wood.

■ Loose screws may also indicate that the hinges are too small or that there aren't enough of them to support the gate. Bent hinges are a sure sign of undersizing. Replace them with the largest size that will fit the gate frame and use the longest screws possible. If the gate has only two hinges, add a third hinge halfway between them. Mortising the hinges into the post and gate provides even more strength.

Sometimes the gate frame itself causes binding. If the hinges are tight and the posts are plumb, make sure the gate is square. An out-of-square or racked gate may require bracing. If the gate-frame connections are weak, you'll need to reinforce them.

■ If the gate structure is weak, you can reinforce the corner joints. First pull the gate square. To do this, measure the diagonals of the frame. Run a pipe clamp along the long diagonal, and tighten it until the diagonals are the same length. Reinforce the gate with a metal bracket or plywood gusset, and fasten any loose boards with galvanized deck screws.

■ To prevent further sagging, attach a wooden brace between the bottom of the hinge side and the top of the latch side. Or you can install a sag rod (with an adjustable turnbuckle, which allows you to correct any future problems) between the top of the hinge side and the bottom of the latch side.

Smart Tip REINFORCE CORNERS

Once you work a racked gate or a section of fence back into square position, there are several ways to secure the alignment. You can add gusset plates made of plywood or add different types of metal hardware. For best results, it's wise to work the gate or fence section slightly past square before you attach any bracing. That way, the stresses that caused the racking to begin with are likely to pull the frame back to square before the bracing takes hold and prevents any further movement.

Square up frames with surface-mounted brackets.

Conceal screws and brackets inside the frame.

Secure corners with decorative plywood gusset plates.

Unracking a Gate

TOOLS
- Clamp
- Framing square
- Power drill
- Measuring tape
- Drill-driver
- Screwdriver bit

MATERIALS
- Lumber for temporary brace
- Lumber for crosspieces
- Screws

1 *Check with a framing square* to see how the frame is racked and which corners are under or over 90 deg.

2 *Apply a pipe clamp,* a band clamp, a temporary turnbuckle, or a come-along to square up the gate.

3 *Add one or more temporary corner braces,* locking up the correct position with screws you can remove later.

4 *One option is to use a diagonal brace* (or two braces in an X-pattern) to reinforce the squared-up frame.

5 *Another option is to install a turnbuckle,* which can be adjusted if the gate racks again.

12

FENCE REPAIRS

Restore a Painted Fence

Wood will last a long time if it is protected from the weather. Once the paint starts cracking and peeling, the first stages of rot will not be far behind. Repainting is easiest if you catch the surface before it deteriorates too much. You can do some light sanding, touch up raw wood if need be, and add a fresh top coat.

It often helps to wash a fence before painting, particularly if the surface is in the shade and has a slightly green tinge from mold and mildew. Surface deposits can reduce paint adhesion.

Many homeowners have power washers that can provide a spray powerful enough to peel old paint. But if the pressure setting is too high, the water stream can dig into wood and erode channels in the softer grain. Always test the pressure on a scrap piece, and adjust the setting and the spray pattern as needed.

If scraping, washing, and sanding expose large areas of raw wood, consider stain instead of paint. It tends to wear away gradually instead of peeling.

Smart Tip LEAD PAINT CHECK

If you need to scrape and repaint an old fence, bear in mind that some paints made before 1978 contain lead, which can be hazardous to your health if you remove the paint without proper precautions. Also, in some areas there are strict codes concerning disposal. If you suspect that a lead-based paint was used, test it with an inexpensive lead-testing kit. Most use a swab sampler (below left) that you apply to a pretreated test card (below right). Even if you scrape and sand only portions of a fence, wear a respirator approved by the National Institute for Occupational Safety and Health (NIOSH), typically one that is certified 99.97% efficient at screening out even microscopic particles.

Restoring a Painted Fence and Gate

TOOLS
- Paint scraper
- Scrub brush
- Pail
- Power washer
- Power sander
- Paintbrushes
- Hammer
- Nail set

MATERIALS
- Exterior paint
- Sandpaper
- Bleach
- Nails

3 **You can use a power washer** *instead of a brush, mixing in a cleaning agent to deal with mold.*

6 **A light sanding** *will generally reduce grain raised by washing. You can belt-sand ornamental gates and posts.*

1 ***Scrape off peeling paint,*** *working with the grain through multiple layers down to bare wood if necessary.*

2 ***Use a stiff scrub brush*** *and a bucket of warm water with a cup or two of bleach to clean off mold and mildew.*

4 ***Power washers can supply a spray*** *with damaging force, so test the pressure on a scrap piece of wood.*

5 ***Check the surface*** *for raised nails, and either set them or pull them and drive new nails or screws.*

7 ***Prime all raw wood*** *with a thinned coat of paint. Spot-prime knots with stain killer to prevent bleeding.*

8 ***Once the prime coat has dried,*** *brush out the top coat of paint, working with the wood grain.*

12

FENCE REPAIRS

Resource Guide

American Fence Association
(800) 822-4342
www.americanfenceassociation.com
The AFA is an organization created to benefit both the fence industry and consumers. Its Web site includes facts about fencing and tips on finding a contractor.

American Hardware Manufacturers Association
(847) 605-1025
www.ahma.org
AHMA is a trade service organization that offers resources for the consumer hardware and home improvement marketplace.

Arch Wood Protection
1955 Lake Park Dr., Ste. 250
Smyrna, GA 30080
(770) 801-6600
www.wolmanizedwood.com
Arch Wood manufactures pressure-treated wood for fences and other items.

Boundary Fence & Railing Systems
(800) 628-8928
www.boundary-fences.com
Boundary manufactures and distributes a variety of fences, railings, gates, and hardware in a multitude of styles, including vinyl and chain-link.

California Redwood Association
405 Entrente Dr., Ste. 200
Novato, CA 94949
(888) 225-7339
www.calredwood.org
This nonprofit association offers general assistance and information about redwood.

Carolina Vinyl Products
P.O. Box 1137
Grifton, NC 28530-1137
(252) 524-5000
www.carolinavp.com
CVP manufactures a line of PVC products, including fences and fence materials.

CertainTeed Corporation
750 East Swedesford Rd.
Valley Forge, PA 19482
(800) 233-8990
www.certainteed.com
Certainteed sells numerous types of building materials, including Bufftech fences.

Chain Link Manufacturers Institute
10015 Old Columbia Rd., Ste. B-215
Columbia, MD 21046
(301) 596-2583
www.chainlinkinfo.org
This institute offers a list of approved chain link retailers and chain-link information.

FenceLink
7040 Avenida Encinas, # 104286
Carlsbad, CA 92009
www.fencelink.com
FenceLink is a directory of fence manufacturers, distributors, and associations for all types and parts of fences.

The Flood Company
(800) 321-3444
www.floodco.com
Flood makes a variety of paint-related products, including penetrating stains, sealers, wood renewers, and cleansers. Visit its Web site for store locations.

Heritage Vinyl Products
1576 Magnolia Dr.
Macon, MS 39341
1-800-736-5143 ext. 2944
www.heritagevinyl.com
Heritage maufactures fencing made from polyvinyl chloride.

Hoover Fence
5531 McClintocksburg Rd.
Newton Falls, OH 44444
(330) 358-2624
www.hooverfence.com
Hoover carries a generous selection of metal, vinyl, chain-link, and specialty fences.

Kroy Building Products
P.O. Box 636
York, NE 68467
(800) 933-5769
www.kroybp.com
Kroy manufactures vinyl fencing and deck materials. It offers free technical advice.

National Ornamental & Miscellaneous Metals Association
532 Forest Pkwy., Ste. A
Forest Park, GA 30297
www.nomma.org
NOMMA will connect you with ornamental metal manufacturers.

National Paint and Coatings Association (NPCA)
(202) 462-6272
www.paint.org
The NPCA is a voluntary nonprofit trade association that represents numerous paint companies.

Ryobi North America
1424 Pearman Dairy Rd.
Anderson, SC 29625
(800) 525-2579
www.ryobitools.com
Ryobi produces portable and bench-top power tools for contractors and DIYers.

Southern Pine Council
(504) 443-4464
www.southernpine.com
Southern Pine Council is a nonprofit trade organization that offers construction tips, complete project plans, and other helpful information on pine and its uses.

Stanco Incorporated
2780 SE 19th St.
Salem, OR 97302
(800) 443-7826
www.stanco-inc.com
Stanco offers a full line of fences, including privacy, decorative, and ranch.

The Stanley Works
1000 Stanley Dr.
New Britain, CT 06053
(860) 225-5111
www.stanleyworks.com
The Stanley Works manufactures an extensive line of hand and power tools.

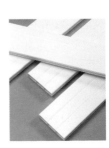

The Vinyl Institute
1300 Wilson Blvd., Ste. 800
Arlington, VA 22209
www.vinylinfo.org
The Vinyl Institute is a U.S. trade association that represents manufacturers and provides information about vinyl.

Glossary

Alkyd paint Often referred to as oil-based, although the oil has been replaced with alkyd resins. It is more expensive, takes longer to dry, and must be cleaned with paint thinner. Alkyd paint is generally considered tougher than latex paint.

Backfill Sand, dirt, gravel, or crushed stone used to fill-in the space around excavation.

Batter boards Horizontal boards set between stakes outside the excavation area used to support layout strings that mark the position of a fence at the start of construction.

Bevel An angled surface, typically cut into the edge of a piece of lumber.

Bowing Warping or bending of horizontal rails (or any lumber) that occurs due to weathering.

Bracing Wood member used to support a structure. In fence building, bracing is usually only temporary.

Building permit A document that may be required for some fence projects, which confirms municipal approval of the proposed construction.

Come-along A hand-cranked winch attached to steel cables and hooks used for many purposes, including straightening fence posts and stretching chain-link fencing.

Dado A rectangular groove across the grain. On fence projects, large dadoes are sometimes cut in wooden posts so that rails can be recessed.

Dry rot Decay from fungi that causes wood to become brittle and crumble to powder.

Finial A decorative element at the top of a post. You can purchase posts with precut finials, cut your own, or purchase separate finials with a screw mount already fitted.

Frost line Depth above which the ground freezes, as recorded for your area by the local building department. Posts must be placed below this line to avoid heaving when the ground freezes.

Galvanized finish Mesh, nails, screws, or other metal materials that are coated with zinc and other chemicals to prevent rusting.

Kerf The narrow slot a saw blade cuts in a piece of lumber, usually about $\frac{1}{8}$ inch thick.

Lag screws Large screws (usually with hex-shaped heads that you turn with a ratchet) used to join wooden fence sections.

Latex paint A water-based paint made up of acrylic and/or vinyl resins and pigments. It cleans up with water and provides adequate protection from the elements in most situations.

Lattice Thin strips of wood that are crossed at right angles or at 45-degree angles, available in pressure-treated wood and colored plastic.

Masonry anchor Galvanized metal fastener, typically with a U-shape and a mounting pin, that is used to hold wood posts on a masonry pier.

Miter A joint in which two boards are joined at angles to form a corner.

Mortise and tenon A type of wood joint in which a hole is cut in one piece of wood, the mortise, to specifically receive the protruding element on another piece of wood, the tenon.

Mounting brackets Metal brackets available in many shapes to fit around the ends of stock lumber. The brackets have predrilled flanges that make it easy to nail or screw wooden timbers to each other.

Overspray Paint expelled from a paint-sprayer that travels beyond pickets, posts, or other targets and can damage nearby grass and plants.

Posthole digger A double-handled tool with shovel-like sides that come together in a scissor-like action to dig post holes.

Prefabricated fence Fence made with posts and panels that are prefabricated of wood, metal, or PVC plastic and come ready to assemble.

Pressure-treated board Wood that has rot-resistant preservatives forced into it under pressure during the manufacturing process.

Privacy fence Fence with solid or almost solid boards used to lend privacy to whatever it encloses.

Rebar Short for reinforcement bar. Metal bars that can be added to concrete piers for added strength.

Spacer board A board ripped to the width between pickets or other repeating components. It is used to make even spaces on a fence.

Subrail A horizontal rail set between the main upper and lower rails that is used to separate fence sections in designs with more than one material, such as a fence with boards on the low section and lattice on the high section.

Trellis A latticework used as a light screen or as a support for climbing plants.

Turnbuckle Hardware with an adjustable eye hook at each end, often set on the diagonal to provide extra support for gates.

Utility fencing Also called snow fencing because it reduces snow drifting, it consists of narrow wood slats held together with wire. It is sold in large rolls.

Welded wire Woven wire mesh available in several grid sizes, often attached to fence posts to act as a trellis for climbing vines or to seal spaces between posts and rails and provide more security.

Index

Photo Credits

Cover: Kotoh/ Zefa/ H. Armstrong Roberts **page 1:** Edifice Photo **page 3:** John Parsekian **page 5:** Phillip H. Ennis Photography **page 6-7:** John Parsekian **page 8:** Jerry Pavia **page 10:** *both* John Parsekian **page 12-13:** *all* John Parsekian **page 14:** Phillip H. Ennis Photography **page 16:** *box* John Parsekian; *bottom* Brian C. Nieves **page 17:** *all* John Parsekian **page 18:** John Parsekian **page 19:** *left row* Brian C. Nieves; *right row* John Parsekian **page 20:** John Parsekian **page 21:** *all* John Parsekian **page 22:** *all* John Parsekian **page 23:** *all* John Parsekian **page 24:** Phillip H. Ennis Photography **page 27:** *all* John Parsekian **page 28:** *left* Brian C. Nieves; *box, top row* California Redwood Association; *bottom row* Stephen Munz **page 29:** *top* Western Wood Products Association; *bottom row* California Redwood Association **page 31:** Garden Picture Library/ Ellen Rooney **page 32:** *all* Merle Henkenius **page 33:** *top* Edifice Photo/ Gillian Darley; *bottom* Merle Henkenius **page 34:** *all* Freeze Frame Photography **page 35:** *top* Edifice Photo/ Philippa Lewis; *bottom* John Parsekian **page 37:** *all* Freeze Frame Photography

page 38: H. Armstrong Roberts **page 40:** *left* Brian C. Nieves *right* John Parsekian **page 41:** Freeze Frame Photography **page 42:** Edifice Photo/ Philippa Lewis **page 44:** Jerry Harpur **page 45:** Freeze Frame Photography **Page 46-47:** *sequence* Freeze Frame Photography **page 47:** *top* Edifice Photo/ Philippa Lewis **page 48:** Brian C. Nieves **page 49:** Robert Harding Picture Library **page 50-51:** *sequence* Brian C. Nieves **Page 51:** *top* Jerry Harpur, designer: Oehme Van Sweden **page 52:** *top* Brian C. Nieves; *bottom* Freeze Frame Photography **page 53:** *top left* Edifice Photo/ Gillian Darley; *top right* Edifice Photo/ Philippa Lewis; *bottom* Freeze Frame Photography **page 54:** Freeze Frame Photography **page 55:** *top left* courtesy of Vermont Fence; *top right* James M. Mejuto **page 56-57:** Kotoh/ Zefa/ H. Armstrong Roberts **page 58:** Brian C. Nieves **page 59:** *top* Brian C. Nieves; *bottom* Jerry Pavia **page 60:** Brian C. Nieves **page 61:** Brian C. Nieves **page 62:** *top left* Jerry Harpur; designer: Edwina Von Gal; *bottom left* Positive Images/ Margaret Hensel; *right* Jerry Harpur; designer: Bob Clark **pages 63-64:** Freeze Frame Photography

pages 65-69: Brian C. Nieves **page 70:** Jerry Pavia **page 72-77:** Freeze Frame Photography **page 78:** *bottom left* Jerry Pavia **page 78-79:** *sequence* Brian C. Nieves **page 80:** *bottom left* Jerry Pavia; *bottom right* Edifice Photo/ Philippa Lewis **page 81:** Brian C. Nieves **page 82:** Tony Giammarino **page 84:** Tony Giammarino **page 85:** Freeze Frame Photography **page 86:** *top* Tony Giammarino; *bottom* courtesy of Stanco **page 87:** *all* Bufftech Fences courtesy of Hoover Fence **page 88-89:** *all* Freeze Frame Photography **page 90-91:** *sequence* Freeze Frame Photography **page 91:** *top* courtesy of Kroy Building Products **page 92:** Jerry Harpur/ Topher Delaney **page 94:** *top* Jerry Pavia; *middle* H. Armstrong Roberts/ H.G. Ross; *bottom* Mike McClintock **page 95:** *all* Jerry Pavia **page 96-97:** Freeze Frame Photography **page 98-99:** Brian C. Nieves **page 100-101:** Brian C. Nieves **page 102-103:** Edifice Photo/ Gillian Darley **page 105:** Freeze Frame Photography **page 106:** *top* John Parsekian; *bottom* Brian C. Nieves **page 107:** *all* Brian C. Nieves **page 108 & 109:** Brian C. Nieves **pages 110-111:** *all* Brian C. Nieves **page 112:** *top* Edifice Photo/ Gillian

Have a home improvement, decorating, or gardening project? Look for these and other fine
Creative Homeowner books wherever books are sold.

Build, step by step, the play structures kids love. 200+ color photos, drawings. 144 pp., 8½"×10⅞"
BOOK #: 277662

Step-by-step deck building for the novice. 500+ color photos, illustrations. 192 pp.; 8½"×10⅞"
BOOK #: 277162

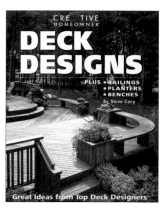

Plans from top deck designer-builders. 300+ color photos, illustrations. 192 pp.; 8½"×10⅞"
BOOK #: 277369

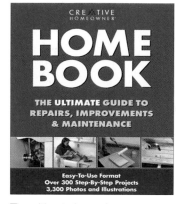

The ultimate home-improvement reference manual. 300+ step-by-step projects. 608 pp.; 9"×10⅞"
BOOK #: 267855

How to build 20 furniture projects. 470+ color photos, illustrations. 208 pp.; 8½"×10⅞"
BOOK #: 277462

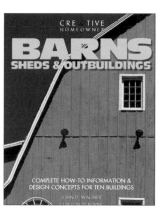

Plan, construct, and finish outbuildings. 600+ color photos, illustrations. 208 pp.; 8½"×10⅞"
BOOK #: 277818

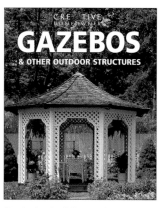

Designing, building techniques for yard structures. 450+ color photos, illustrations. 160 pp.; 8½"×10⅞"
BOOK #: 277138

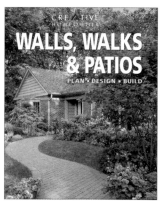

Build landscape structures from concrete, brick, stone. 370+ color illustrations. 192 pp.; 8½"×10⅞"
BOOK #: 277994

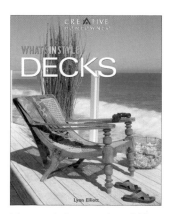

Newest designs, products. 200+ color photos. 128 pp.; 8½"×10⅞"
BOOK #: 277183

Idyllic at-home getaways. 200+ color photos. 128 pp.; 8½"×10⅞"
BOOK #: 279456

Impressive guide to garden design and plant selection. 600+ color photos, illustrations. 320 pp.; 9"×10"
BOOK #: 274615

Lavishly illustrated with portraits of over 100 flowering plants; 500+ color photos. 208 pp.; 9"×10"
BOOK #: 274032

For more information, and to order direct, call 800-631-7795; in New Jersey 201-934-7100.
www.creativehomeowner.com

Darley *right* Brian C. Nieves **page 113:** Brian C. Nieves **page 114:** *top* John Parsekian; *bottom* Freeze Frame Photography **page 115:** Brian C. Nieves **page 116-117:** Freeze Frame Photography **pages 118-119:** Jerry Pavia **page 120-121:** *bottom* Freeze Frame Photography **page 121:** *top* Jerry Pavia **page 122:** *top* Jerry Pavia **page 123:** *top left & top right* Freeze Frame Photography; *middle left* courtesy of Garden Iron; *middle right* Jerry Harpur, designer: Oehme Van Sweden **page 124:** Freeze Frame Photography **page 125:** *top* Marcus Harpur; designer: Andy Rees, UK; *bottom* John Parsekian **page 126-127:** Jerry Harpur, designer: Edwina Von Gal **page 128-129:** *sequence* Freeze Frame Photography **page 129:** *top* John Parsekian **page 130:** *top* Freeze Frame Photography; *box, top left* Dr. James Jarrett, Mississippi State University, Dept. of Entymology; *box, top right* John Parsekian; *box, bottom left & right* Agricultural Research Service **page 131 & 132:** Brian C. Nieves **page 133:** Freeze Frame Photography **page 134:** *box* Brian C. Nieves *right* Freeze Frame Photography **page 135:** Freeze Frame Photography

Metric Conversion

Length

1 inch	25.4 mm
1 foot	0.3048 m
1 yard	0.9144 m
1 mile	1.61 km

Area

1 square inch	645 mm²
1 square foot	0.0929 m²
1 square yard	0.8361 m²
1 acre	4046.86 m²
1 square mile	2.59 km²

Volume

1 cubic inch	16.3870 cm³
1 cubic foot	0.03 m³
1 cubic yard	0.77 m³

Common Lumber Equivalents

Sizes: Metric cross sections are so close to their U.S. sizes, as noted below, that for most purposes they may be considered equivalents.

Dimensional lumber	1 × 2	19 × 38 mm
	1 × 4	19 × 89 mm
	2 × 2	38 × 38 mm
	2 × 4	38 × 89 mm
	2 × 6	38 × 140 mm
	2 × 8	38 × 184 mm
	2 × 10	38 × 235 mm
	2 × 12	38 × 286 mm
Sheet sizes	4 × 8 ft.	1200 × 2400 mm
	4 × 10 ft.	1200 × 3000 mm
Sheet thicknesses	¼ in.	6 mm
	⅜ in.	9 mm
	½ in.	12 mm
	¾ in.	19 mm
Stud/joist spacing	16 in. o.c.	400 mm o.c.
	24 in. o.c.	600 mm o.c.

Capacity

1 fluid ounce	29.57 mL
1 pint	473.18 mL
1 quart	1.14 L
1 gallon	3.79 L

Temperature

(Celsius = Fahrenheit – 32 × ⅝)

°F	°C
0	–18
10	–12.22
20	–6.67
30	–1.11
32	0
40	4.44
50	10.00
60	15.56
70	21.11
80	26.67
90	32.22
100	37.78